Jeremiah
The Iron Prophet

G.T. Dickinson

Southern Publishing Association, Nashville, Tennessee

This book was
Edited by Don Short
Designed by Mark O'Connor
Cover design by Bob Redden
Cover photo by Doug Brachey

Type set: 9/11 Palatino

Printed in U.S.A.

All Bible references are taken from the Revised Standard Version, unless otherwise indicated. All references to the Book of Jeremiah are given without the use of the name as (2:24).

Other translations used are:

KJV—King James Version

NEB—The New English Bible. Copyright, The Delegates of the Oxford University Press and The Syndics of the Cambridge University Press, 1961, 1970. Reprinted by permission.

Library of Congress Cataloging in Publication Data

Dickinson, George T
  Jeremiah, the iron prophet.

  1. Jeremiah, the prophet. 2. Bible. O.T.—
Biography. 3. Bible. O.T. Jeremiah—Criticism,
interpretation, etc. I. Title.
BS580.J4D5 224'.2'06 78-15455
ISBN 0-8127-0183-6

Contents

Chapter 1

A MAN FOR TODAY

The Essence of Life:
"A rarer spirit never did steer humanity" (Shakespeare).

The prophet of gloom and doom? Don't you believe it.

Jeremiah deserves a better image. His spiritual quality and moral responsibility were awesome. Negative? Perhaps. But constructively and progressively negative, like wind that blows the smog away. Do not be turned off by the mention of his name. His exciting life is dramatically relevant today.

Jeremiah was a realist—a man who recognized bad conditions and then spoke the truth with powerful conviction. He did not sit under a fig tree out in the quiet countryside playing a harp while Jerusalem burned. Always where the action was, he courageously and unselfishly shared the trials and sorrows of the people who often scorned him. He turned religion from a nationalistic creed into an intense personal experience.

Jeremiah's life and times have a special meaning today. Troubled Judah, plagued by corruption, venality, rampant violence, and loss of virtue, resembled the world we live in. Jeremiah fearlessly pointed out the wrongs and then prescribed the only cure. But there existed a subtle strain of joy and hope in his dramatic calls to repentance.

This great man was a person of flawless integrity and intense loyalty—first to God, then to his countrymen. There is evidence that the Babylonians would have favored him, but he remained behind in ruined, bitter Jerusalem, among his difficult friends and defiant enemies. When a pro-Egyptian party led the Jews into Egypt, contrary to his advice, he went along, even though the leaders of the conspiracy despised him. He didn't lack courage.

The great prophet is a man for today and should be heard by modern men, mired in many of the muddy situations that troubled Jeremiah and his people. In relevancy he could be called the prophet who lives again.

We first see the young future prophet standing among the fig and olive groves of Anathoth, three miles northeast of Jerusalem, looking down into the furnace of the Jordan valley. He is thankful for his cool, bracing upland home. But the easy, gentle days did not last. He was destined to feel the hot breath of opposition and hate, the fury of men bent on doing evil.

Keep in mind that the chapters of Jeremiah do not follow chronological order. They are arranged on another basis—just as are books of the Old Testament. For example, Ezra and Nehemiah are placed in the historical section. If appearing in time sequence, they would be near the end of the Old Testament among the minor prophets.

The chronological order suggested by *The Seventh-day Adventist Bible Commentary* will be followed in this book:

"Josiah (639-608): chs. 1-6; 14-16.

Jehoiakim (608-597): chs. 17; 7-11; 26; 35; 22:1-19; 25; 18-20; 36:1-4; 45; 36:5-32; 12.

Jehoiachin (597): chs. 22:20-30; 13; 23.

Zedekiah (597-586): chs. 24; 29-31; 46-51(?); 27; 28; 21; 34; 32; 33; 37-39.

After the fall of Jerusalem: chs. 40-44; 52" (Vol. 4, p. 348).

You will like Jeremiah. It is inspiring, stimulating, captivating, a choice piece of sacred literature with a powerful message for today. We ought to know this remarkable man better. Out of the agony of the iron furnace his searching mind opened the glorious prospect that God listens to every worshiper. His living convictions become food and drink for our souls today. Through him we catch marvelous glimpses of the Messianic radiance and a thrilling vista of celestial wonders awaiting the redeemed of all the ages.

Jeremiah shows us how the man of God is moved by a profound sense of awareness. His soul is deeply touched by responsibility toward God. He keenly feels the pain and suffering soon to overcome the people he loves. It is a costly thing. Leila Bagley Rumble in her booklet, *A Guide to a Study of Jeremiah*, says, "So many of us live only in the middle range of the scale of life. We never know the full range of living because we limit our thinking and our feeling to the areas of life which we can accept without pain.

"Today we see Jeremiah as a man deeply sensitive to the sins of his people and to his responsibility for their sins. He found that he could not feel deeply without doing something about it. Knowledge is necessary as a basis for feeling, and feeling is necessary as a basis for action.

"There is a story of a man who, when walking over a Scottish moor, picked up a moss cup and began to examine it under a pocket lens. A shepherd, seeing what he was doing, became interested and was allowed to see the flower through the glass. 'Can this be a moss cup?' he exclaimed. 'I wish you had never shown it to me!' When the man asked, 'Why?' the shepherd replied, 'Because I tread on thousands of them every day.

"As we come to know the evils in which we live, and feel that they are wrong, we should do something about them. Blum's Almanac tells farmers when to plant and when to expect the 'unsettled spells' and adds that the best place to pray for a good crop of corn is between the rows, and while using a hoe."

Jeremiah's prayers were persistent, and he offered them amid hostile rows of obstinate opponents in Jerusalem, using the hoe of God's reproof upon the weeds of apostasy.

By exploring the world of Jeremiah you are about to begin a thrilling experience. It could rejuvenate flagging zeal so evident among Christians today and replenish the spirit of heroic witnessing. Here, indeed, is a towering figure waiting vicariously to step into your life.

Jeremiah, seldom at a loss of nerve and spiritual strength, always stood on the firing line of moral resolution. He reminds us that truth and our responsibility are forever indivisible.

Chapter 2

THE BOLD ONES DO IT

The Essence of Life: One learns to do the will of God by *doing it*.

Jeremiah, a man of absolute integrity, could not be bought at any price. Moreover, he could be counted on to do a job no one else wanted. You can imagine his taking a shovel and cleaning out the barn when his associates suddenly found themselves busy with other tasks.

His book in the Bible begins with, "The words of Jeremiah." That says enough. Whatever this amazing man spoke was the unqualified, unvarnished truth. When God asked him to say something that people were sure to resent, he never tried to tone it down.

"Couldn't you just look the other way and save your neck?" friends would urge.

"Not when God tells me otherwise."

He could hear God's word because of a receptive mind and heart. Thousands of others *said* their prayers and attended the Temple, but his fervent worship conditioned him for the prophetic call. The revelation of a holy and majestic God absorbed his whole being, and he did not ask for an easy job, but just to do the Lord's will.

Moreover, his candid, frank attitude came well blended with integrity of the highest order. He refused to compromise principle the way some are doing on the extramarital front today.

Openly indulging lax standards, such as sleeping together in apartments or spending weekends at home in the same room, many college students, tacitly condoned by indifferent or "open-minded" parents, say they are looking at life honestly and truthfully instead of hypocritically. "We indulge; why not let the truth be known instead of hiding it like hypocrites?" they say.

The same attitude—using the excuse of frankness—goes for a number of modern indulgences: immodesty in dress, sex talk, lax conduct among married couples, for instance.

Jeremiah used adultery as a figure to express the most reprehensible departure of a guilty people away from God and into idolatry. "You defiled my land," cried the prophet (2:7). He called for truth, candor, forthrightness. He did so on the very highest moral elevation of blameless, Ten Commandment living.

Clean, pure, honest, elevated words were the kind Jeremiah directed at a people who didn't want that kind of talk. But he kept on telling them without nonsense, double meaning, or diplomatic whitewash.

To guilty people he points an accusing finger, "How can you say, 'I am not defiled'? . . . '[You are like] a wild ass . . . sniffing the wind, . . . [unable to] restrain her lust' " (2:23, 24).

Yet all of this brave, fearless rhetoric came the hard way. It was not in his nature to stand up and take on the whole world filled with sneering, contemptuous people whose greatest joy would be to hang him on a tree for the birds to pick apart. Timidly he shrank from the divine charge.

"Ah, Lord God! behold, I cannot speak: for I am a child," he pleaded (1:6, KJV).

If he had been overconfident or boastful, God could not have used him. So his weak point became his strongest point. They who soar too high and far on their own wings get to where a sudden blast often rips them apart.

"Humility, that low, sweet root

   From which all heavenly virtues shoot" (Thomas Moore, *The Loves of the Angels*).

Nor did Jeremiah parade that pride which apes humility. He knew what it meant to be a prophet: there would be long hard days, great distinction but bitter battles. He would rather live a quieter life more in keeping with his retiring nature than become an exposed cedar on the heights of Lebanon. But God liked what He saw in the young man.

"The Lord said unto me, Say not, I am a child: for thou shalt go to all that I shall send thee, and whatsoever I command thee thou shalt speak. Be not afraid of their faces: for I am with thee to deliver thee, saith the Lord" (1:7, 8, KJV).

Little imagination is needed to enter into the feelings of a sensitive young man around twenty years old who, surrounded by the soft beauty of Palestine, ardently loved a peaceful life. True, the spiritual condition of his people caused him anxiety when he thought about it, but the exuberance and optimism of youth overshadowed such thoughts. Yet the versatility of this unusual man blended easily into a passionate loyalty to Israel's God, so he listened eagerly when the mystic voice spoke to him.

Gone, in one sweeping command were hopes and plans for an easy comfortable life of possible material advantages, prospects of a happy marriage and a pleasant home. Almost instinctively, knowing the moral condition of the nation, he sensed it meant the hard task of defying his countrymen, both high and low.

Jeremiah, when God made him an anointed instrument, became a formidable being, ready to challenge Judah's travesty: a crude caricature and rank distortion of the true faith. His high sense of honor, selfless devotion, and unwavering fidelity made him one of the most distinctive men of the age. Yet he hesitated when the call came.

"Lord, I don't know what to say," one can almost hear him plead. "There are men who can tell it much better. Why don't You use them?"

But God was not looking for eloquence, talent, or brilliant personalities. He wanted a man with passionate love for truth, a man of probity who could be trusted in fair weather or foul. Given these, God could use the man—He would amply supply the needed resources.

"See, I have this day set thee over the nations and over the kingdoms, to root out, and to pull down, and to destroy, and to throw down, to build, and to plant" (1:10, KJV).

God gave him a stunning challenge, something that would have quailed his heart had the call been anything but a divine order: "I will utter my judgments against them touching all their wickedness," declared God (1:16, KJV).

The young prophet knew what this meant. He would be the one who must give the unwelcome announcements. If he still had lingering doubts about the difficulties that lay ahead, God cleared these up.

"But you, gird up your loins; arise, and say to them everything that I command you. Do not be dismayed by them, lest I dismay you before them. And I, behold, I make you this day a fortified city, an iron pillar, and bronze walls, against the whole land, against the kings of Judah, its princes, its priests, and the people of the land. They will fight against you; but they shall not prevail against you, for I am with you, says the Lord, to deliver you" (1:17-19).

Today it would be something like telling a housewife, proud of her cooking, that she is feeding her family the wrong food and that she should do some reading on the subject of nutrition. Or like denouncing a man who boasts about the sharp deal he made, or a young woman telling her wolfish date to shape up or get out.

In other words, God told Jeremiah right at the beginning that he could not expect to be a popular preacher. There would be plenty of trouble and some very unpleasant reactions to the messages he must bear.

"Throw him out!" would be a term cast at him more times than he could number. Catcalls, vulgar remarks, false accusations, brickbats, rotten apples, and flying eggs came his way more often than he liked to think about. But God promised to take care of His faithful servant. Jeremiah was ready for anything as long as he had the assurance of God's approval and guidance. To serve his Maker meant everything. Running around gathering the effervescent favors of men, as the false prophets and priests were doing, disgusted him greatly.

James A. Froude, a noted English historian, in *Oceana* tells of meeting the gardener while on his way to visit Sir George Grey, the governor of New Zealand. What were his pastimes, asked Froude: hunting, fishing, riding, etc.?

"None."

"What, then, do you like?" asked Froude a little testily.

"I like being servant to Sir George Grey."

Jeremiah could have said the same about the Lord. Youthful delight in the sheer act of living, the infectious wholesomeness of his character, became completely absorbed in the sober realities of a heavy prophetic office. God's plans and purposes, as in the life of every person who yields to divine guidance, stood out clear and distinct above everything else.

"Go and cry in the ears of Jerusalem," came the order from above (2:2, KJV).

The city of David, exquisitely attractive to every Hebrew, was subtly stimulating. Aside from being the religious and political center of a nation and a religion, new forms of experimentation had created a false sense of exuberance. Political developments fanned a feeling of excitement. But any discerning person could read below the superficial surface of the bubbling city and experience an uneasy feeling of revulsion. On the better side a great reformation, led by one of the good kings, now challenged the disgraceful apostasy of former reigns. Yet the city needed a prophet who would tell the straight truth.

Jeremiah was instructed to remind the nation of God's bountiful dealings in the past—the way the people had been led out of Egypt, through the wilderness, and into the Promised Land.

But how quickly have a favored people forgotten their Benefactor and turned to idols. "Be astonished . . . at this, and be horribly afraid" (2:12, KJV).

What is this foolish thing an ungrateful people have done, this act of absurd folly?

"For my people have committed two evils; they have forsaken me the fountain of living waters, and hewed them out cisterns, broken cisterns, that can hold no water" (2:13, KJV).

God has glorious plans, but the human element always mars His benevolent purpose. His perfect church is filled with imperfect people, some of whom turn from the fresh sparkling fountain of crystal water to the brackish, bitter, stagnant pools of this world.

Let us say (as Jeremiah intimated) the people tire of their pure water. Possibly the bubbling spring is some distance away, and the effort required to bring the water into town upsets their desire for ease. They shirk from the sacrifice, disdaining the rare, pure spring. So they call a town meeting.

"Let's dig a well nearby," urges one of the citizens.

All agree, except one or two, who find themselves hopelessly outvoted. Becoming remarkably busy, the people start digging with surprising zeal, but their work turns out to be very shoddy. The result is a cistern, not a well of fresh water. And there is a crack in the bottom, which makes it unsatisfactory. Then, obsessed by their cistern mentality, the townspeople dig more holes with the same results. All the while they neglect the perennial spring where water is sweet and abundant.

Jeremiah is instructed to tell these deluded people what God thinks of them. "It is an evil thing and bitter, that thou hast forsaken the Lord thy God" (2:19, KJV).

Imagine the young prophet during this early springtime in his life walking about the city, still optimistic that most of the people will listen to him.

He meets a priest.

"You're the one who claims to be a prophet, eh?"

"The word of the Lord came to me."

"Well, well," muses the old priest. "How do you know it was the Lord? Maybe you have just been hearing voices."

"God gave me visions."

"Visions?"

"Yes. I saw an almond tree in full bloom."

The priest enjoys needling the young man, thinking he is one of the overzealous types springing up on the lunatic fringe of fanaticism. He asks what happened then, a slight twisting of his lips indicating a degree of cynicism.

"The Lord spoke to me. I saw a seething pot and fire."

"Pray, what did that mean?" asks the priest in mock surprise.

"God told me that disaster would come upon this land."

The priest advises Jeremiah to go home and pray over the matter. "Young man, when God is ready to reveal these things to us, some of the older priests also will have visions. Until then, I advise you not to disturb the people."

Such a confrontation would have come as a shock to the young prophet, even though he expected skepticism, even hostility.

"It is the very essence of all right faith," says Ellen White, "to do the right thing at the right time." The bold ones, who do not scream, "Hurricane!" when a leaf flutters, do this. Jeremiah was the kind—one of the authentic bold ones. There is something grand and heroic about the scene as the young prophet fearlessly walks into Jerusalem with a vital message from God: "You cannot prosper while living in sin; throw away your mask of hypocrisy;

drink from the pure fountain." He met fierce resistance.

It is true to life that anyone who keeps God's commands will often meet misunderstanding, ridicule, and contempt—even among his friends. But on the other hand a man's lifetime is only a very faint whisper in the vast immensity of time and eternity. We are not put here to gather sweet comforts and effervescent praise. The challenge of life confronts us with a vast dimension of mission reaching into eternities that nothing on earth can even begin to measure.

At the same time there filters through Jeremiah a tender, sensitive spirit, a strong strain of love, hope, and courage, which the whole sorry confused world desperately needs.

Chapter 3

THE GOLDEN YEARS

The Essence of Life: "His word was in mine heart as a burning fire shut up in my bones, . . . and I could not stay" (20:9, KJV).

Jerusalem has always been a place of supercharged history, a crystallization of hope and glory, a vision of beauty. On the other hand it often harbored ghettos of misery, cynicism, and rebellion.

So let us listen to a possible dialogue on one of her streets:

"They're singing and waving palm branches up around the Temple."

"What's going on?"

"The king has told us we're going to have a revival."

"A revival? It's about time—there isn't an honest person here."

One man, a landowner, didn't have much faith in the city people, nor did he like the turn toward idolatry his countrymen had taken. The other, a tradesman, knew the city well and could report almost everything that went on within its sturdy walls.

"There's a young prophet from Anathoth," said the tradesman, "who's cutting a straight line right up to the king's palace."

"Oh? That is something new."

The tradesman nodded, a smile creasing his canny face. "And the king is listening to him."

"Hm-m. I'll have to go and listen to him myself."

When Jeremiah received his first vision, Josiah, one of the best kings who ever reigned in Jerusalem, had been on the throne for about thirteen years. Since he was eight when his reign began, this would make him twenty-one years old at the time the prophet had his first vision, or about the same age as Jeremiah.

It seems logical that both worked together in promoting a revival of religion, although neither the books of Chronicles and Kings nor Jeremiah mention the fact. One reference, however, is suggestive. At the death of Josiah after a reign of thirty-one years 2 Chronicles 35:24, 25 says, "All Judah and Jerusalem mourned for

Josiah. Jeremiah also uttered a lament for Josiah."

It would seem most extraordinary if the reform-minded king gave no heed to the provocative words of the prophet. One can read between the lines and discover parallel interests leading to the same high objectives which surely must have drawn the two young men together. Truth, precious and divine, formed a rich pearl both men prized supremely. The ragged, twisted ways of the nation, riddled by falsehood, were more than either could bear.

Akbar, greatest of the Mogul emperors in India, once said, "I have lived a long time, but I have yet to see a man lost on a straight road." *

The straight course of revival was running strong in the royal court when Jeremiah appeared on the scene. Both young men undoubtedly thrilled as the work of reformation spread through the land. Jeremiah could well rejoice, even though he had no other choice but to point out the shallow extent of repentance in the public consciousness. God did not allow him the luxury of complacency in the golden years of spiritual prosperity.

Leaping the centuries the same voice calls the Laodiceans before the triumphant return of Jesus: "For you say, I am rich, I have prospered, and I need nothing; not knowing that you are wretched, pitiable, poor, blind, and naked" (Revelation 3:17).

God is not going to give His people rest until the work is complete. No superficial, half-done, careless, lukewarm attitude will do. It didn't pass under Jeremiah's honest scrutiny any more than in the time when John's words will apply to festering wounds of hypocrisy, lukewarmness, and superficiality.

So amid the general upsurge of ecstasy, the songs, the praise, the prayers, a young prophet took the podium and sounded an alarm.

His inherent tact suggested a preamble lauding their response to the growing spiritual appeal, before going on to point out the necessity of greater depth. But God had not included any softening-up preliminaries in His instructions, and Jeremiah was so completely dedicated to the message God gave him that he could not add such either. He never would think of saying, "Well,

---

Golden Treasury, p. 314. Droke House. Indianapolis, 1955.

after all, it's just a little thing. God isn't going to be all that particular about unnecessary details."

You hear such excuses offered today: "It doesn't matter which day one keeps, just so he keeps one."

"But the commandment defines the day of rest."

"Oh, that—well, it's just a matter of interpretation."

Or someone else comes up with freewheeling permissiveness:

"Dances, theaters, a glass of beer—— Would God shut people out of heaven because of these little restrictions? Come on, now! Don't be a legalist."

On this point Jeremiah stood as solid as Mount Moriah. He could never be found rationalizing, temporizing, or compromising. If he had to tell his best friend that he was a knave, the young prophet donned his cloak and lost no time getting there to deliver the unwelcome report.

There came to Jeremiah, a man of peace, the painful duty of telling the people that their religion was a sham. God instructed him to use the case of a wife leaving her husband for trysts with illicit lovers. Will a man take her back? Then he went on to talk about the wayward sisters, Israel and Judah, steeped in harlotry, who polluted the land with their adulteries. Though an outraged husband could not be expected to take back a wife who turned harlot, yet God promises mercy to guilty people. His love, compassion, and forgiveness extend to the vilest of sins. Listen to the sweet tender appeal as Jeremiah poetically puts it:

> "Return, faithless Israel,
> says the Lord.
> I will not look on you in anger,
> for I am merciful,
> says the Lord;
> I will not be angry for ever.
> Only acknowledge your guilt,
> that you rebelled against the
> Lord your God. . . .
> Return, O faithless children" (3:12-14).

The appeal comes through loud and strong. God loves His wayward, backsliding people. Like children, they are disobedient and rebellious, but the fountain of mercy runs full. Jeremiah, the iron prophet of stern rebuke, makes the message crystal clear: God's unmistakable purpose is to take back the worst of sinners—even those as bad as a wife deserting her husband and becoming a prostitute. The worse the sin, the broader His mercy.

A tramp—dirty, unshaved, ungodly, totally destitute—came into New York and began begging on the streets. What makes a tramp? How does he become one? This man had left a home of comfort and ample means to wander about in his deplorable condition. Perhaps there had been misunderstandings or discipline he resented. Whatever it was, he had yielded to the fury boiling within his soul, and as a result became an outcast, living on the crumbs of society.

One day he asked a man for ten cents. When the man turned to give him a dime the beggar saw the face of his father.

"Why, you're my father. Don't you know me?"

The wretched condition of the son made it difficult at first to recognize him, but in a minute the father knew he had found his lost child.

Throwing his arms around him, he cried, "My son, my son, I have found you! All I have is yours!"

Jeremiah gave a similar message to Jerusalem. Going into the guilty city, he told the people they were religious beggars and harlots. Their pride resented the charge. Here they were, having somewhat of a national revival. They were rich—so they thought—in their spiritual possessions and increase of goods. Now comes this young fellow from nowhere and tells them they are backsliding children, perverting their ways. Preposterous!

Some responded, and to Jeremiah's satisfaction the work of reform took on deeper tones as far as they were concerned. But others, proud and vain in their lukewarm state, resented the upstart from the country. They didn't want to be disturbed. So they continued like vagabonds and harlots. And Jeremiah continued to tell them just what kind of people they were. He diminished no reprimand.

But he interspersed warm bursts of hope and promise with his candid appraisal of the situation. In other words, Jeremiah said, "Now listen to me. I'm not going to compliment you when you don't deserve compliments, but let me emphatically tell you that

there are some wonderful things ahead if you repent and turn
from your backsliding."

In the poetic portion of chapter three is this beautiful appeal:

"I said, How gladly would I treat you as a son,
        giving you a pleasant land,
            a patrimony fairer than that of any nation!
    I said, You shall call me Father
        and never cease to follow me.
    But like a woman who is unfaithful to her lover,
        so you, Israel, were unfaithful to me.
        This is the very word of the Lord. . . .
    Come back to me, wayward sons;
        I will heal your apostasy" (3:19-22, NEB*).

Jeremiah, wishing above everything else to see a wholehearted
response to his message, stands at the gate telling himself that the
offers of God, the supernal benefits of doing things His way are so
wonderful there should be one grand rush into the bright shining
pathway. He puts the words they should speak into their mouths:

"O Lord, we come! We come to thee;
    for thou art our God.
    There is no help in worship on the hill-tops,
        no help from clamour on the heights;
    truly in the Lord our God
        is Israel's only salvation.
        From our early days
        Baal, god of shame, has devoured
        the fruits of our fathers' labours,
    their flocks and herds, their sons and daughters.
Let us lie down in shame, wrapped round by our dishonour,
        for we have sinned against the Lord our God,
        both we and our fathers,
        from our early days till now,
        and we have not obeyed the Lord our God" (3:22-25, NEB).

The appeal is almost pathetic. We see the picture of a loving

*From The New English Bible. Copyright, The Delegates of the Oxford University
Press and The Syndics of the Cambridge University Press, 1961, 1970. Reprinted by
permission.

Father, willing to provide every blessing, pleading for His un-grateful, debauched, sin-loving children to come home to His paternal house of joy and plenty. But there is a trace of reality in the pleading voice: "Will they do it? Will they turn from their evil ways and love Me?" He wants to give them everything—far more than all they have now—if they will only love Him.

As Jeremiah pressed his plea, many responded sincerely to his call. Even a few of the indifferent and lukewarm stayed to listen whenever he delivered his strong appeals at the gate. Word prob-ably came to him that his work had impressed the king. He drove home the point that God is supremely interested in people's welfare and is only waiting for them to come into the warm fold of love.

"If you will but come back, O Israel,
  if you will but come back to me, says the Lord,
  if you will banish your loathsome idols from my sight,
      and stray no more . . ." (4:1, NEB).

Encouraged, the young preacher tells them how to penetrate the mystic curtain of repentance and encounter the glowing pre-sence of divine favor. "Break up your fallow ground," he urges in verse 3.

How, Jeremiah? How does one break up the fallow ground?

His answer would have been the same then as today. Take the hand of God. Live wholeheartedly for Christ. Instead of a few meaningless words muttered without enthusiasm, pray as though it were a direct encounter with God and life depended on it. Make first things first. A field of rich soil that could produce beautiful flowers and choice food lies unused. Plow the ground, and plant the seeds of righteousness. Then share the rich harvest with others.

Chapter 4

THE KING AND THE PROPHET

The Essence of Life: Sustaining, energizing faith comes only by a close connection with God.

Josiah the youthful king and Jeremiah the young prophet wore the same brand of reform sandals. Both strode into the apostasy scandal and began to clean up the corruption that blighted the country.

Nineveh, long an oppressor of Israel, had gone into decline before the rising power of Babylon, leaving a political vacuum in Israel, the northern kingdom, which Josiah largely filled. Competent and totally dedicated, he was now free to become involved in spiritual matters, which he took on with great enthusiasm.

Coming to the throne at eight years of age, Josiah evidently had fallen under early influences for good. Zephaniah the prophet, because of his noble blood, probably had access to the child king. The prophets Habakkuk and Huldah also were known at court, especially the latter. Then, of course, Jeremiah added his powerful voice to those whom the king no doubt respected. Though the iron prophet preached a doomsday scenario, his tough mind often yielded to a tender heart and a loving, sensitive spirit that the responsive king likely appreciated.

Nothing better has been written about a king than that on Josiah: "He did what was right in the eyes of the Lord, . . . and he did not turn aside to the right or to the left" (2 Chronicles 34:2).

Attitudes toward the old religious faith made for total contrast between father and son. Of Amon, Josiah's father, we have the record: "This Amon incurred guilt more and more" (2 Chronicles 33:23).

What caused the difference between the two kings? Both had the same opportunities, the same knowledge of truth. But Josiah used his opportunities; he placed faith and the pursuit of truth above everything else. He simply said no to the strange fascination of Baal that attracted so many of Judah's kings. Thus Amon

21

became a minus figure in history while Josiah, possessing an astonishingly strong character and sense of direction, became a star in the constellation of greatness. The new king stood almost alone.

"Run to and fro through the streets of Jerusalem," declared God to Jeremiah. "Look and take note! Search her squares to see if you can find a man, one who does justice and seeks truth" (5:1). It seemed as though the whole city had turned against God.

When Josiah reached the age of sixteen, something happened that caused him to seek the Lord with intense devotion (2 Chronicles 34:3). We do not know what triggered his upward thrust. He began to ask himself some searching questions:

"What is God trying to tell me? How can I better serve Him? Are there some things I have neglected to do?"

Maybe he pondered the words of the prophet Zephaniah (the great-great-grandson of King Hezekiah), who probably appeared quite often in the palace. Declaring the word of the Lord, the prophet said, "I will stretch out my hand against Judah" (Zephaniah 1:4). Zephaniah may have repeated to the boy king God's call to repentance:

"Seek the Lord, all you humble of the land,
> who do his commands;
seek righteousness, seek humility;
> perhaps you may be hidden
> on the day of the wrath of the Lord" (Zephaniah 2:3).

When Josiah set his heart toward seeking the Lord, he soon became aware of the extent to which his kingdom had departed from the true faith. All about him were the conditions Jeremiah would denounce a few years later. "Their transgressions are many, their apostasies are great" (5:6). Jeremiah would also pinpoint the moral degeneracy that attended the decline of faith. " 'How can I pardon you?' " asks God (5:7). He had filled them with great abundance, but they used their peace and plenty, their leisure time, in illicit pursuits.

"They committed adultery and trooped to the houses of harlots. They were well-fed lusty stallions, each neighing for his neighbor's wife" (5:7, 8).

The displeasure of God over such moral relapses was to be

marked out by the words God would soon command Jeremiah to speak: " 'Shall I not punish them for these things?' " (5:9).

Yet in spite of the warnings voiced by the existing prophets and those soon to be delivered by Jeremiah, the people paid little attention. "Business as usual, and a good time in our spare time," seemed to be the universal attitude.

One can see the prevailing state of mind as God has a dialogue with the human race.

" 'The house of Israel and the house of Judah have been utterly faithless to me. . . . They have spoken falsely' " (5:11, 12).

The usual response in those days (today too?) and what God would do about it can be summarized from 5:12 through chapter 6.

"God loves us too much to punish us. No evil will come upon us. These doomsday prophets are just bags of wind."

The prophet answers them by quoting God: " 'Behold, I am making my words in your mouth a fire, and this people wood, and the fire shall devour them.' " A nation shall attack the land. The sword will destroy this fair country.

" 'Hear this, O foolish and senseless people,

who have eyes, but see not,

who have ears, but hear not.' "

But the people are stubborn and rebellious. They listen instead to their false teachers. Wicked men, expert at defrauding others, become great and rich. They grow fat and sleek at the expense of other people. Evil seems boundless throughout the land.

"An appalling and horrible thing

has happened in the land;

the prophets prophesy falsely,

and . . .

my people love to have it so."

"It's coming," warns Jeremiah. "Blow the trumpet! Evil looms out of the north. Prepare war! The Babylonians are coming!"

But the people do not listen to the weeping prophet. The false prophets oppose him, and the priests cry, "Peace, peace" when there is no peace.

There is no malice on Jeremiah's part. He wants them to take heed, to come back under God's protection and gentle care. Again he quotes God:

> " 'Stand by the roads, and look,
>   and ask for the ancient paths,
>   where the good way is; and walk
>   in it,
>   and find rest for your soul' " (6:16).

The response is negative. "We will not walk in it." In other words, they have a streamlined, modernized religion. Go back to the old ways? "Don't be absurd. This suits us much better."

Nonetheless, the invitation to repent stands. God wants His people to enjoy the best things in life; therefore, He warns them of the consequences if they choose a contrary course. God takes no pleasure in the misery of the wicked, but He doesn't stop a man who is bent on destroying himself. The proof of His benign purpose is implicit in the analogy appearing at the close of chapter 6.

God tells Jeremiah that he is to be like an assayer. Such an individual is always seeking real values among the rock specimens sent to him. If you sent a piece of ore from a mine on your property and the assayer reports back $1,000 to the ton, you would have a bonanza.

Once we sent a specimen to be assayed. The silver content ran high. "You better get in and develop that property," advised the assayer.

He had separated the valuable mineral from the worthless material. This represented the work of Jeremiah. His words sounded harsh to unbelieving ears, but he dealt with the refining fire that would bring out the valuable metal from the worthless country rock.

"The bellows puff and blow, the furnace glows;
    in vain does the refiner smelt the ore,
  lead, copper and iron are not separated out" (6:29, NEB).

Sometimes it may seem rather difficult to catch the harmony, the beauty hidden within the stern warnings of Jeremiah. Yet it is there. The use of an assayer proves the point. He employs fire to bring out the valuable material. No one would spend time and money digging a hole in the earth just for rock that has no value. In every mining camp an assayer proves a valuable citizen indeed. God, for man's good, also seeks quality.

Many times samples, over which a miner cherished fond dreams, proved disappointing when put to the test by the assayer. One can imagine the disappointment of a prospector who put too much hope on a piece of ore that did not measure up to his expectations. On the other hand, there have been very rich mines shunned, ignored, and passed over by even experienced miners where someone later found a promising vein. The assayer confirmed its worth by his unfailing standard of testing. The fabulous Kelly Silver Mine at Randsburg, California, is an example. Booted feet of experienced prospectors tramped over it scores of times until someone tested an outcrop. It produced millions.

If a piece of rock could talk, it might say, "I don't like all this pounding and hot fire. It hurts."

"Little rock," replies the assayer, "this is the only way to find out if you are worth anything."

Sometimes gold is so well disseminated in the ore that the eye cannot see it. The assayer, however, proves it to be rich in the yellow metal.

God tells Jeremiah that "a great nation is stirring from the farthest parts of the earth. . . . They are cruel and have no mercy" (6:22, 23). Judah, no longer allied with God, would not be protected as in former times.

The refining fire would have one purpose only: to purify, to separate the dross that marred the nation. Men such as Daniel and his companions would emerge from the fiery testing "more precious," as Isaiah 13:12 (KJV) puts it, "than fine gold."

Several years remained before Jeremiah's words of doom were heard in the land. Now, at the age of sixteen, Josiah, the royal penitent, felt the warm impulse of spiritual revival flowing in his soul. He offered earnest prayers. Nearby in a quiet village another teenager, a future prophet, prayed with the same fervor. Both were on the threshold of stirring events, and the two would blend their efforts in promoting a great revival, the last before the guilty, backsliding nation went down in utter ruin.

A crisis calls for men of valor who take firm steps in the right direction without counting the cost. Usually they save the day and bring a glow of satisfaction into life that no compromise or soft lethargy can ever provide.

Josiah, about to take some bold steps, will rock the nation and send the false teachers scattering like rabbits when the hounds appear.

And Jeremiah—young, fearless, full of zeal for the ancient faith—will be waiting to greet the horsemen of Josiah when they ride into Anathoth. Steel will meet steel and be sharpened by the contact. The centerpiece of Josiah's campaign will be to reorganize the whole nation on the old religious lines. Every time he opened the closet doors around the Temple, a new scandal dropped out.

"This will never do," Josiah must have repeated many times. "I'm going to clean out this moral corruption if it takes all my troops to do it."

No doubt Jeremiah heard about the reforming zeal of the king and wholly supported it. One can almost hear him say, "If the royal guard comes to Anathoth, I'll welcome them with open arms."

Some of his acquaintances, indulging the lax ways of Baal permissiveness, probably said, "We hope they leave us alone."

"Ah," we can imagine the young Jeremiah replying, "I think they're coming, and it's about time to do something about this scandal."

Looking at the uneasy Baal lovers, he could have commented with a sly twinkle in his eyes, "I saw an officer from the court in town the other day. You'd better start running right now."

Chapter 5

THE VIRGIN DAUGHTER
IS SMITTEN *

The Essence of Life: When something drastic needs to be done, zealous men will do it.

"Throw them out! Smash Baal!"

All Judah feels the iconoclastic zeal of Josiah. The young king sends his officers throughout the country to stamp out the degraded cult of Baal.

Now in the limelight on center stage: a drastic drive stirs the entire land to banish the demoralizing system that has profoundly weakened the nation.

It sounds as if Josiah started the campaign by a dramatic gesture. Let us construct a probable scene around the bare facts of the case as we find them stated in 2 Chronicles 34:4: "And they broke down the altars of the Baals in his presence."

A crowd gathers at the sect's temple, with its sacred tree, in Jerusalem—the king wants the event well publicized so his subjects will get the message that subversion must go.

His majesty appears. High officers of the court, accompanied by assistants carrying hefty mauls, follow him.

"Break it down," orders the king.

Avidly his servants go to work. Idols are smashed, masonry flies about, curtains are ripped apart. The wreckers rip and smash and pulverize, gaining zest as the grim wrecking party continues. Thus begins an important campaign in the life of Josiah, the smasher, king of Judah.

Since he was a good Hebrew devoted to the purity of the faith, it was logical that the young king would come to this. Now twenty, having matured into a wise, prudent ruler, Josiah has become wholly dedicated to the proposition that he is a chosen

---

*This chapter based on 2 Chronicles 34:3-7 and Jeremiah 14.

defender of the faith. The movement quickly spreads from Jerusalem as royal officers, accompanied by armed guards, ride from city to city. Their explicit purpose is to purge the land of Baal, the corrupter. Soon the whole kingdom feels the rolling thunder of the smasher as molten images are reduced to dust. Incense altars come down. The bones of dead priests, superstitiously venerated, are hauled to the altars and publicly burned to powder.

The campaign does not change the essential direction of compromise and apostasy, but it checks the downward rush. Subversion in many places goes underground, confident the reforming zeal will in time burn off. Many of the leaders, always ready to drift with the tide, give lip service to the drive, for it is now a popular national policy. They are the prophets who will become some of Jeremiah's most bitter antagonists. In a dialogue God and His prophet discuss these teachers.

We now go from chapter 6 to chapter 14 in order to follow the accepted chronological sequence. Here God declares He will not accept the halfhearted repentance of the people (14:10, 11).

Josiah is leading in the right direction, but the response lacks real sincerity. There is fasting and praying, but it is a mere form without a significant change of heart.

Jeremiah tries to excuse the misguided people. The leaders are confusing them, he claims. They are promising, "You shall not see the sword; all is going to be peace and security."

The Lord answers Jeremiah, who has given this recital of what the leaders are saying: "The prophets are prophesying lies in my name; . . . worthless divination, and the deceit of their own minds" (14:14). He informs Jeremiah that they themselves will be consumed by the very sword and famine they claim will not come.

These men had mixed fact and fancy, truth and error, Baal and Jehovah, to such a bewildering extent that the people had become utterly confused, usually following the way best suited to their natural inclinations. Thus we have the background of conditions in Judah when the young smasher undertook his drastic action and Jeremiah pronounced the oracles of doom.

In an interview on the "Today" show, a sports editor questioned the editor of a new magazine—one that has zoomed to a phenomenal circulation and is aimed at serious intellectual readers—about the accuracy of an article on baseball. When presented with inaccuracies in the article, the editor of the prestigious magazine readily admitted the errors but explained that the misstatements were seriously used merely to provoke thought. In his estimation, accuracy did not have the highest priority.

Such attitudes also prevailed in Judah during Jeremiah's time. Honesty, truth, integrity, were no longer national characteristics. Insistence on the absolute truth, uncorrupted by subtle introductions of Baalism, did not meet with universal support. The leaders were not noted for preaching righteousness, the glory of seeking truth in its purest forms. "Both prophet and priest ply their trade through the land, and have no knowledge" (14:18), accused Jeremiah.

We would hardly recommend Josiah's method for dealing with apostasy today. But times were different: Judah, a theocracy, enjoyed direct revelations of God's will and had to maintain civic order as well as religious purity.

About a year after Josiah's campaign had begun, Jeremiah received his first vision. He lived in Anathoth, three miles northeast of Jerusalem and pleasantly situated on a site overlooking the deep Jordan valley. Walking among the fig and olive groves, for which Anathoth was noted, Jeremiah as a youth felt early promptings of intense devotion to the ancient faith. The trees followed the system and order of Creation far better than his people. Not once did a fig or an olive corrupt its appointed destiny by trying to be something else or by bringing forth a different kind of fruit. By contrast some of the priests in his town had incorporated elements of the Baal cult into Hebrew worship. Instead of holding steadfastly to simple uncluttered worship, they had introduced parts of the elaborate, sensuous forms of Baal, beginning with what seemed harmless little details. In time Baal worship held more and more attractions, especially as it offered a freer, uninhibited, permissive way of life.

Young Jeremiah didn't like it or the other open-end developments in social relaxations. Before Josiah struck, people were getting more careless about the way they handled truth—a tendency man always contends with when the standards begin to fall. Careful attention to detail was overlooked. But Jeremiah went about the pursuit of truth with the tenacity of a laboratory technician or a research doctor—no details were unimportant.

Possibly Jeremiah's concern for the details of truth created trouble for him in Anathoth. He became an object of dislike for something he did, was driven out of town, and told not to come back. It could have begun with the idol-breaking crusade, nursed quietly by those affected, and then brought to the surface when Josiah's days were over.

It would not be out of character for young Jeremiah to have said, "Straighten out your devious ways, sweep the place clean of all your Baal corruption, or I'll take the troops right to your secret rooms behind the synagogue curtains when the king's housecleaners come this way."

Likely (if this did happen), some old heads reluctantly nodded but swore vengeance on the young zealot. Jeremiah's remarks, surely very penetrating, came from an effective agent who could always be relied upon to tolerate nothing but the strictest purity and undeviating truth. A dangerous crowd in priestly robes, it is true, had got hold of things almost everywhere in Israel, and now they were met by one who could never stand hypocritical subversion.

So comes the day when Josiah's men ride into Anathoth. They are met at the town gate by a young man, his eager sensitive face catching the penetrating eyes of the officer. In a firm, convincing voice the youth says, "We are clean inside. Come, inspect our place." Of course we are still imagining it happened this way.

During the period of Josiah's cleanup a severe famine ravaged the land. Jeremiah says much about it in chapter 14.

Perhaps the severity of the famine persuaded Josiah to intensify his drive against idolatry.

" 'Judah mourns,' " cries the young prophet. " 'The ground . . . is dismayed' " (14:2, 4).

Possibly several years have passed since he was given his first vision, and now he is a confirmed prophet with national stature. No doubt he already has interviewed the king and advised him. Josiah's attitude inspires him to pray for deliverance:

"Though our sins testify against us, yet act, O Lord, for thy own name's sake. Our disloyalties indeed are many; we have sinned against thee. O hope of Israel, their saviour in time of trouble" (14:7, 8, NEB).

He suffers with his people. Probably he and the king have agreed that the work of repentance has not gone deep enough, the Baal mentality is still lingering in superficial attitudes. They conclude that the idolatry crisis has endangered the nation because God cannot bless falsehood and hypocrisy.

> "Let my eyes stream with tears,
> ceaselessly, day and night.
> For the virgin daughter of my people
> has been broken in pieces,
> struck by a cruel blow" (14:17, NEB).

There was only one way out of Israel's dilemma: zeal for God. He alone could heal the stricken nation. Halfhearted measures were not enough. Only the all-out zealous methods Josiah and Jeremiah employed can save a nation or a person in such desperate circumstances. Such enthusiasm puts flavor, hope, and sparkle into life. Now Josiah was ready for another leap forward, and Jeremiah awaited the divine oracle as a continuing work of national reform progressed.

Have we too sought the source of conquering faith?

In what do we put our trust?

Only a life that depends on God will meet our needs.

The test of time has proved the utter inadequacy of all else. How deep is our religion? We must feel as well as think.

Chapter 6

LOST TREASURE AND A PROPHET'S CONFESSION

The Essence of Life: Every person *can* hear God's call.

"Evil shall break forth," cried Jeremiah, pressed to speak by the prompting of God.

A sense of mystery overshadowed him. He told about the dark side of living in falsehood and about the bright side of dying, if need be, for truth. He bent every effort to prevent an unspeakable human tragedy.

Sensitive, incorruptible, fearless, he told his people a terrible disaster would befall the land unless they took more seriously the call to repentance and separate forever from the whole rotten system of Baal.

"Pestilence, sword, famine, captivity! It's all coming unless drastic changes are made," warned the prophet. Jeremiah 15:4 puts the finger on the one man most responsible for the unhappy situation—Manasseh, the son of Hezekiah. The worship of Baal, the pollution of the mind and the soul, had been received by the confused, headstrong son of a good king. He slid into all the fantasies, depravities, and twisted delusions of idolatry with greater fanaticism than even the heathen themselves.

He promoted Babylonian star-worship, Molech with its repulsive rites of human sacrifice, and Ashtaroth or Astarte (the Greek Aphrodite), the naked goddess of sex worship, with temple prostitutes included. Thus a mingled religion of idolatry and the Hebrew faith spread through the land.

Moreover, Manasseh's wild orgies filled the capital with violence. He "shed very much innocent blood, till he had filled Jerusalem from one end to another" (2 Kings 21:16). Finally God said he had gone too far—judgments so severe that ears would tingle at the news would fall on the guilty king.

That is exactly what happened when the armies of Assyria

struck with irresistible fury. Then Manasseh, carried captive to Babylon, finally repented. Restored at length to his throne, he tried to undo some of the evil he had wrought in Judah. But the fascination of idolatry was too strong to root out, and his son Amon, the apostate father of Josiah, lapsed back into heresy during his short reign.

Now history was again to repeat itself. Jeremiah's exquisitely poetic appeals and eloquently pathetic warnings were the final plea to a doomed nation so saturated with the Baal perversion that the case seemed hopeless, even though Josiah stemmed the downward plunge for a while. Jeremiah's reference to Manasseh, no doubt, indicated the same use of trouble to straighten out the moral condition of the Jews at this time.

In fact, adversity has done much to enrich the human race. Many men who would have been satisfied if rich became great because adversity taught them the rugged virtues of life.

Etude magazine tells of a young composer complaining to Johannes Brahms, one of the supreme masters of music, about the poverty that made it difficult just to purchase manuscript paper. The great musician then showed the young man the original writing of his famous *Requiem*. The paper did not match. "I could not afford to buy a lot of the same paper at any one time," he explained.*

The sole purpose of the troubles God sent to Israel was to refine, to bring out the beauty and melody of righteousness.

Josiah, however, having chosen the same wise course that Hezekiah (his great-grandfather) followed, did not plunge his country into the troubles caused by apostasy. Six years after starting the great reformation, in the eighteenth year of his reign, he began to repair the Temple in Jerusalem and in doing so made a startling discovery.

Someone, poking around in the trash accumulated during years of neglect, discovered a priceless copy of probably a portion of Deuteronomy, by Moses. After this book of the law was read to him, the king reacted vigorously, launching out into another dramatic move in his continuing work of reform (2 Chronicles 34).

---

*Quoted in *Golden Treasury* (Droke House, 1955), p. 8.

What we see happening in Jerusalem is an example of cause
and effect, a sequence of actions that led to wholly desirable ends.
Reformation inspired the rebuilding of God's house, which in
turn led to a discovery of the holy book. Then (as we shall see in
the next chapter) the sacred book prompted an expansion of the
revival, with resulting benefits extending in many directions.

During these years of hope and glory, Jeremiah continued to
voice the will of God—he exhorted, reproved, counseled, and
sometimes wept. Without doubt the work of Josiah pleased him,
but an uneasy feeling persisted that what was good in itself would
in time prove insufficient. The Baal mentality had captivated the
popular fancy, and the average man found it difficult to come back
into the simple faith, unadorned by sensualism and voluptuous-
ness.

So Jeremiah frowned at times. Maybe there existed at times
some irritation in the mind of Josiah: the prophet seemed to
downgrade the popular revival. Yet their admiration for each
other remained strong.

Jeremiah wanted people to like him, but he had to say things
that ignited resentment and created hostility. All this drew heav-
ily on his physical and spiritual resources. Evidently the growing
dislike for him caused a temporary lapse in his zeal for God.
Instead of being alienated and put out of the mainstream, he
wanted respect and friendship. So he stopped talking and began
complaining:

"Alas, alas, my mother, that you ever gave me birth!

a man doomed to strife, with the whole world against me.

I have borrowed from no one, I have lent to no one,

yet all men abuse me.

The Lord answered,

But I will greatly strengthen you;

in time of distress and in time of disaster

I will bring the enemy to your feet" (15:10, 11, NEB).

These verses are typical of the pathetic longing, the keen desires, of the misunderstood man, who wanted to be a friend of
every man. He wept day and night, his tender soul wounded
beyond consolation at times (14:17).

Let us listen in to parts of Jeremiah's confession during his conversation with God. He wants to please his Maker, but he simply can't take all of this dislike, the wagging fingers, the scorn, any longer.

" 'Be patient with me,' " he pleads with God. Then to paraphrase: "Don't you see: it's too much for any man—leave me alone for a while."

"See what reproaches I endure for thy sake. I have to suffer those who despise thy words" (15:15, 16, NEB).

But in the midst of his complaining, the prophet concedes that God's word to a faithful man creates supreme joy in the soul. "Thy word is joy and happiness to me" (15:16, NEB).

Yet unhappy thoughts of self-pity return, and he continues the refrain of complaint.

"I have sat alone, . . . my pain unending, my wound desperate and incurable" (15:17, 18, NEB).

He blames God for abandoning him to the indignation of perverted men: "Thou art to me like a brook that is not to be trusted, whose waters fail" (15:18, NEB).

Why do good men suffer when God is supposed to care for them? Expand the question—why do all men suffer?

Rogers in *Jacqueline* has the answer:

"The good are better made by ill,
As odours crushed are sweeter still."

An Associated Press story reported that the New Jersey "salad oil king" released from prison was a chastened, slimmer man.

"Coming here actually saved my life," Anthony de Angelis, convicted of a $150 million salad-oil fraud, told newsmen. He had used forged warehouse receipts as collateral to borrow money. His business venture collapsed, leaving some of the nation's big banks holding the bag.

As he left the penitentiary, De Angelis said, "I came here weighing 250, and I leave at 170. Spiritually, physically, and morally this prison has saved my life."

His confession reflected the purpose of corrective discipline—contrasted to punitive punishment—and how one should feel about it: "I have no sorrow for coming here. I did wrong, and I paid the penalty."

In dealing with a guilty backsliding nation God used adversity for the same purpose. Even Jeremiah, a most pious man, needed to be trained; hence God understood the moments when he felt lonely and forsaken. The voice from heaven brought gentle reproof and assurance.

"If you will turn back to me, I will take you back
        and you shall stand before me.

    If you choose noble utterance and reject the base,
        you shall be my spokesman" (15:19, NEB).

God told him there would be more opposition, but he would be made impregnable, "a wall of bronze." What He told the prophet is a promise all men may enjoy when hard pressed, discouraged, and misunderstood.

"They will attack you but they will not prevail,
        for I am with you to deliver you
            and save you, says the Lord;
    I will deliver you from the wicked,
    I will rescue you from the ruthless" (15:20, 21, NEB).

After all the joys and sorrows, the ups and downs, the endless vicissitudes of life—as Jeremiah knew them—there is just one thing that really counts: What kind of a man comes out of the refinery. Perhaps Jeremiah cried, "Lord, I want to be appreciated instead of scorned all the time. Give me some people who like me."

But God did not often send this kind across his path—although there must have been many in Judah—because the prophet had to be honed by hostility and adversity for his great mission.

The real Jeremiah, whose life is the essential story of true men through the ages, has been obscured by a misconception of his nature. All the gentle, loving instincts within him were thrust into the stern reality of confrontation and hostility and misunderstanding.

The remarkable thing in his book is that it tells us more of what we need to know about ourselves and our own challenges. Anyone who has felt the urge to give up and flee away from it all will know the struggles of Jeremiah. He found his way out of discouragement. We shall have to find ours.

Chapter 7

STANDING ALONE

The Essence of Life: "Too long the darkened way we've trod; Thy truth, O Lord, send down" (*Christian Worship and Praise*, p. 430).

Jeremiah, disgusted with city ways and incorrigible people, walks out one balmy spring morning to his home in Anathoth. There he hopes to find a few quiet hours away from the suspicion, the hostility, of unfriendly city dwellers and temple priests. His reception in Anathoth proves typical of what he can expect everywhere.

In our imagination we see him arriving at home, met not by the former warmth of a close-knit, loving family but by a degree of tenseness and reserve.

After the customary greetings, Hilkiah, the father, introduces a subject much on the mind of the family—in fact, something of special interest to the whole town.

"Your preaching—those predictions—they're beginning to affect your reputation. You had better not say anything at the gate this time."

"Reputation? I'm sorry, Father, but reputation means nothing to me. I'm concerned only with God's will."

Hilkiah, a priest in Anathoth (one of the towns assigned to Levites), is very sensitive to news that comes from the Temple in Jerusalem; some of it bodes ill for Jeremiah. "Just the same," he firmly replies, "you don't have to do all your doomsday preaching around here."

" 'These are the words of the Lord,' " declares Jeremiah, repeating the words God had given him: " 'I have withdrawn my peace from this people' " (16:5, NEB).

"My son," interrupts the prophet's mother, "you can tone it down. For our sake, please. It's getting embarrassing for us."

"I'm sorry to embarrass you," replies Jeremiah, "but when God speaks, I must obey."

"That doesn't preclude common sense," pontificates Hilkiah.

The son again repeats words God has given him as an example of what he must say: "In this very place, I will silence all sounds of joy and gladness, and the voice of bridegroom and bride" (16:9, NEB).

Hilkiah abruptly changes the discussion. "Bridegroom and bride—that's another thing I want to talk about."

His frown has changed to a sly smile, the kind one imagines a cat has when it corners a mouse.

"Of course you remember old Kohath's daughter."

"Oh, yes—Miriam," replies Jeremiah. "A lovely girl. There's none better in all the country."

"You were playmates together," coos the mother, "and there was always a sort of understanding between the families that someday the two of you would——" Her voice trails away into an ethereal murmur.

"Well, the point is this," affirms Hilkiah. "Kohath and I have talked it over. He will put up half his olive grove with half of mine and that will be our dowries. Such a fine grove would make just about the best piece of land between here and Jerusalem."

"But," objects Jeremiah, "with all this prejudice and talk they would never think of it."

"Just give them a chance. After all, they have always been very fond of you. And Kohath even told me the other day he thought you might be right."

"Shall your father and I go over right away and talk about it?" inquires the eager mother.

"No."

"What did you say?" explodes Hilkiah. "No one in his right mind would turn down such an opportunity."

Jeremiah quotes one of his visions. "The word of the Lord came to me: You shall not marry a wife; you shall have neither son nor daughter in this place" (16:1, NEB).

Hilkiah springs to his feet. "You're crazy, stark crazy!" he roars. "Go back to Jerusalem and spout your visions, but keep quiet around here." (This is implied rather than recorded.)

It's hard for men to learn that God means what He says. By now Jeremiah had learned well, but few others in Judah gave much heed to God's will. Even one of life's richest and finest arrangements—a pleasant home—must be denied the prophet because his strong affections and sympathies might weaken the iron in his soul during the trying days ahead.

In the meantime Josiah, having heard the curses pronounced in the rediscovered book of the law, written by Moses, became thoroughly alarmed. Sending a delegation to Huldah the prophetess, he inquired if the judgments Moses cited would come upon the nation. The court must also have called to mind Jeremiah's persistent warnings of the same fate. Huldah confirmed that the judgments were certain to come, but Josiah would be spared since he had repented—disaster would come after he had passed from the scene (based on 2 Chronicles 34:19-33).

"Repent! Repent!" cried the king to his subjects. A great meeting of many thousands was called at Jerusalem. Very likely Jeremiah attended and added his voice to the insistent appeal of the king. At least we assume he was there.

Possibly voices from Anathoth and Jerusalem came to him with tempting suggestions at this time of national revival. An act of accommodation, an innocent word of appeasement—certainly not a surrender of principle—would make his life tolerable and even pleasant, while in the eyes of the nation his honor would remain untarnished.

One can be sure he found himself tempted by such suggestions, for after all he remained a human being desirous of goodwill. The sublime surely stretched thin at this point, and one must admire the courage of a man who could continue to draw the contempt of almost everyone when a single word would win favor and popularity.

The warning, however, continued strong and clear, unfaltering as he spoke for God: "My eyes are on all their ways; they are not hidden from my sight, nor is their wrongdoing concealed from me. I will first make them pay in full for the wrong they have done" (16:17, 18, NEB).

Pollution of the soul, a serious condition among the Jews, called for a drastic change. The hearts and minds of men can become as corrupted as the environment they often pollute. No half measures can hope to solve either the problem of the soul or that of the environment.

I think of the rivers of Oregon, where we spent many pleasant years. I recall an enjoyable swimming interlude on beautiful Clackamas River, rising in the forested Cascade Mountains and flowing uncontaminated into the lush Willamette Valley and the river of the same name.

Our wives drove three of us up the Clackamas and then met us downstream after we turned boys again, splashing, floating, laughing, and swimming in the clear, smooth water, dashing through a swift current here and there. For us it was pure juvenile joy again, made possible by the clear water and charming scenes along the way.

But in the past decade the lovely rivers of Oregon, especially the Willamette, have been threatened and sometimes made shockingly foul by man-made wastes. The state took the matter seriously in hand, and the *National Geographic* paid "tribute to Oregonian tenacity in pushing through the most successful river-rejuvenation program in the country" (*National Geographic*, June, 1972, p. 818).

The rotten, filthy, polluted river presented a gigantic challenge, but the cleanup campaign plugged away. Industrial waste came under severe control. Beer cans disappeared, and riverside clutter became a thing of the past. Now the river is regaining its unspoiled charm, and swimming is safe once more.

But the ambitious progam cost millions, requiring the enthusiastic participation of the populace and strict control backed by constant vigilance. "A lot of little efforts," said Tom McCall, Oregon's governor who spearheaded the drive, "make the big difference between success and failure" (*ibid.*, p. 834). Now the state is driving toward transforming the 510 riverbank miles along the entire length of the beautiful Willamette into a continuous green-way park system.

Since the scent of the devil hung heavy over Palestine, Jeremiah dedicated himself to combating the pollution of men's hearts and souls. At first people humored him, then ridiculed him, and finally resented him. Yet he did not change one word or qualify a single prediction.

Forewarned, Jeremiah would find the people grossly overestimating their piety. He was told they would say, " 'Why has the

Lord pronounced all this great evil against us? What is our iniquity? What is the sin that we have committed against the Lord our God?' '' (11:10).

Superficially the question appeared reasonable. It seemed to them that Jeremiah was overstating the case in view of the revival sweeping the land. But the answer to their protestations of innocence came clear and emphatic. They had forsaken the law and departed farther from God than their fathers. They refused to listen, following instead their own stubborn wills.

They were swept into the enthusiasm of the religious awakening without a real change of heart. '' 'Therefore,' '' says God, '' 'I will make them know my power and my might' '' (16:21).

Genuine religion is far more than crying, "Lord, Lord." It is a teachable attitude, listening to the voice of God in the soul and carefully heeding the will of the Lord.

Chapter 8

CAKES FOR THE QUEEN OF HEAVEN*

The Essence of Life: "Choose this day whom you will serve, . . . but as for me and my house, we will serve the Lord" (Joshua 24:15).

Like a mechanic trying to fix an old car, Jeremiah strove desperately to correct the spiritual malfunctions of his countrymen.

As he concentrated on the objective, his crystal sincerity made itself felt. He was on fire to rectify social and religious iniquities and to defend the ancient faith. "The heart is deceitful above all things, and desperately corrupt," he cried; "who can understand it?" (17:9).

Yet with his searching indictment there also came a delicate sense of justice and hope that sprang from his own feeling for basic needs of the human soul and the potential dignity of man.

"Blessed is the man who trusts in the Lord,
     whose trust is the Lord.
He is like a tree planted by water,
     that sends out its roots by the stream,
and does not fear when heat comes,
     for its leaves remain green,
and is not anxious in the year of drought,
     for it does not cease to bear fruit" (17:7, 8).

This shows the prophet, having denied himself the pleasure of owning trees, appreciating their value in measuring the worth of a man. Palestine had a variety of trees to gladden and serve man, but nothing like California, where endless types—from the graceful palm to the stately redwoods—grow profusely.

Everyone has heard of the redwoods or the giant sequoias growing along the northern coast or in the Sierra Nevada mountains, but few know how they were named. These greatest of trees

---

*This chapter based on Jeremiah 17:7, 8; 2 Chronicles 35.

commemorate a remarkable half-blooded Cherokee Indian named Sequoya, the only man in history known to have developed an entire alphabet.

An accomplished silversmith and painter, unable to speak English, he received a severe wound while serving in the U.S. Army, and it crippled him for life. But the misfortune made him great, for he now turned to a life of thought and study.

"Why is the white man superior? Ah," said Sequoya, "the secret is his ability to talk on paper."

Painstakingly the Cherokee went to work on a dream to educate his illiterate, dying people. For twelve years he experimented while onlookers ridiculed and sneered at the dreamer. But in 1821 he gave the tribesmen an amazing alphabet of eighty-six letters—superior to the English alphabet—which enabled anyone who spoke Cherokee to read and write it after a few days of study.

Gospels were printed, then a tribal newspaper, and finally a constitution for the now-rejuvenated "Cherokee nation."

No longer jeered at, Sequoya had created a sensation. Finally men conceived the idea of dedicating to his memory one of the finest monuments ever designated for man: the great trees that had sheltered Indians long before the white man came. The noble trees would forever bear the name of a patient man who invented a remarkable alphabet on the barks of trees.

Speaking of the great trees, John R. White, former superintendent of Sequoia National Park, wrote: "It is their astounding age, as well as their size and beauty, which fills the soul of puny man with awe and reverence for the Creator" (the *National Geographic Magazine*, August, 1934, p. 219).

Having compared a man who trusts in the Lord to the enduring trees, Jeremiah declares the just ways of God. "O Lord, the hope of Israel" (17:13), he cries.

But some ridicule him; feeling secure and complacent, they sneer at his predictions: "Where is the word of the Lord? Let it come!" (17:15).

God sends His faithful servant, scorned and misunderstood but undeviatingly true to his sacred charge, among the people at the gate to proclaim the word of the Lord.

"Take heed for the sake of your lives!" (17:21) he warns in

vehement words, stopping men in their tracks. That they are liberalizing the old landmarks is his specific charge.

"Do not carry a burden out of your houses on the sabbath or do any work, but keep the sabbath day holy, as I commanded your fathers" (17:22) is God's message that Jeremiah now drives home.

If the day of rest, proclaimed amid the fires of Sinai and made forever the standard of worship by inclusion in the Sacred Ten, is observed, then, says Jeremiah, Jerusalem will stand a glory and a praise among the nations. Chariots and horses, kings and princes, will come, the sweet incense of frankincense will float through her streets, and she shall live forever. Jeremiah warns, " 'But if you do not listen to me, to keep the sabbath day holy, [then nothing but disaster will fall upon the nation]' " (17:27).

What happened?

"They did not listen or incline their ear, but stiffened their neck, that they might not hear and receive instruction" (17:23).

At some time during the period when these words were spoken, a crushing tragedy struck the nation. Josiah, the reforming king, was killed. Then began the dark years of renewed apostasy and national confusion that led to final collapse.

The generally accepted historical corollary now takes us from chapter 17 back to chapter 7 and onward to 11.

"Amend your ways!" (7:3). Jeremiah, voicing the call with fervor, shakes a few but only irritates many.

"We've heard that before," say the unbelieving sort, tired of listening to what they think is the prophet's incessantly negative preaching. But the Anathothite is a realist. He knows there is only one way to stave off the threatening disaster; so along with his warnings he points to the only solution.

As a curtain raiser, the son of Josiah came to the throne only to be deposed after three months by the Egyptians, who then appointed his brother Jehoiakim. This young king proceeded to undo the work of Josiah his father—"he did what was evil in the sight of the Lord" (2 Chronicles 36:5). The whole nation supinely followed him.

With all their heathen innovations and dishonest ways, popular fancy still clung to the concept of a chosen people, the favored of heaven: "my creed, my race, my Temple."

Jeremiah demanded, "Do not trust in these deceptive words: This is the temple of the Lord, the temple of the Lord, the temple of the Lord' " (7:4).

In other words, don't run to the Temple when the enemy comes—it isn't going to do you any good. Just turn to the Lord and see how wonderful it will be for you.

"For if you truly amend your ways and your doings, if you truly execute justice one with another, . . . then I will let you dwell in this place, in the land that I gave of old to your fathers for ever" (7:5-7).

"Hypocrites, all of you! You say you're on God's side, and all the time you steal, murder, commit adultery, swear falsely, and burn incense to Baal. You've made the house of God a den of robbers by your presence! What can you expect?" cried Jeremiah.

The prophet tells them that God will demolish everything, Temple and all, as He did at Shiloh. Now, if that isn't enough, God cites the supreme insult to His name. "Do you not see what they are doing in the cities of Judah and in the streets of Jerusalem?" (7:17).

It's the queen-of-heaven outrage!

"The children gather wood, the fathers kindle fire, and the women knead dough, to make cakes for the queen of heaven" (7:18).

Evidently this corruption was especially offensive to God; it vexed the soul of Jeremiah like a hot needle to his flesh. The worship of both Ishtar, the Assyro-Babylonian female deity, and the Canaanite equivalent, Astarte, combined grossly immoral practices with its debased ceremonies. Now the Hebrews were mixing these practices with their pure Jehovah worship. No wonder the prophet declared, "Truth has perished" (7:28).

Jehoiakim (609-598 BC) became deeper and deeper involved in the defiling practices of Baal. Jeremiah denounced the nation as perpetually backsliding.

"How can you say, 'We are wise, and the law of the Lord is with us'?" he asks (8:8).

He is telling them not to fool themselves. It would be the essence of common sense to look at matters candidly and stop trying to be something one isn't. Along with departure from the pure faith comes the attendant vices: "From the least to the greatest every one is greedy for unjust gain; from prophet to priest every one deals falsely" (8:10).

It can be reasonably inferred that the tenacious Anathothite did not exactly relish the work of denouncing his countrymen, but it had to be done; and since God had given him the task, he did not shirk his duty.

Carl Sandburg relates an anecdote Lincoln told that goes something like this: A friend asked the chief executive how it felt to be President of the United States. Lincoln recounted a tale about a man tarred and feathered and ridden on a rail. When a bystander asked him how it felt, he replied that if it were not for the honor conferred upon him, he would rather walk.

While Jeremiah, had he consulted his feelings, would have chosen another course, he nonetheless continued to tell his people how wrong they were, simply because God asked him to do it.

"Were they ashamed? . . . No, they were not at all ashamed; they did not know how to blush" (8:12).

> "When I would gather them, says
> the Lord,
> there are no grapes on the vine,
> nor figs on the fig tree;
> even the leaves are withered,
> and what I gave them has passed
> away from them" (8:13).

There is nothing cynical about Jeremiah. He doesn't say, "Wait and see, then you'll hear me gloat, 'I told you so.' " Not the prophet. What he saw coming pained him beyond words.

> "My grief is beyond healing,
> my heart is sick within me.
> Hark, the cry of the daughter of my
> people: . . .
> 'The harvest is past, the summer is
> ended,
> and we are not saved.' . . .
> I mourn, and dismay has taken
> hold on me" (8:18-21).

One man has the courage to stand in the breach as the defenses go down. Jeremiah's resolve to speak for God marked him as a man who had chosen a dangerous but magnificent course. In the final determination, man's Great Judge will honor such heroism. He will look men over for the scars of honorable battle, not the glittering medals of armchair strategists who shirk the struggles of life.

Refined in the fire of His Spirit, Jeremiah came out pure gold. Perhaps as much as any man in sacred history, he can inspire us today with the heroic image of those who belong wholly to God.

Misunderstood in his day, he has been honored by following generations as one of the greatest of the prophets. God always vindicates His man, if not in this world, then certainly in the next. Time proved Jeremiah. He did not live to hear the acknowledgments of men, but he didn't seek human approbation anyway. Longfellow said, "Man is unjust, but God is just; and finally justice triumphs."

A just vindication of Jeremiah is reflected in Dr. H. C. Case's estimation: "He more nearly anticipated the gospel of Christ than any other teacher in the old dispensation" (*The Prophet Jeremiah*, p. 15).

Chapter 9

GOLD FROM UPHAZ *

The Essence of Life: The grass keeps growing up no matter how many times you cut it.

Only one thing has absolute substance. All things else are mere images on a phantom screen.

The life of Josiah proved one substantial, incontestable fact: serving God with the whole heart brings success, prosperity, security, and eternal life. The deplorable record of his successors, with all the confusion, falsehood, and impiety, proved a mere phantom of life leading to trouble, disaster, and oblivion.

Jeremiah planted the flowers, but the aphids of Baal soon blighted them. He kept cutting the grass, but it always came up again. No matter how hard he tried to keep down rampaging apostasy, it kept pushing up. Stay with them and weep, or run away from it all—these thoughts preyed upon the mind of the frustrated, sensitive seer.

> "O that my head were waters,
>> and my eyes a fountain of tears,
> that I might weep day and night
>> for the slain of the daughter of my people!
> O that I had in the desert
>> a wayfarers' lodging place,
> that I might leave my people
>> and go away from them!
> For they are all adulterers,
>> a company of treacherous men.
> They bend their tongue like a bow;
>> falsehood and not truth has
>> grown strong in the land;
> for they proceed from evil to evil,
>> and they do not know me, says the Lord" (9:1-3).

---

*This chapter based on Jeremiah 9-11.

Ironically, catering to the gods of the heathen gave the nation no favor in the sight of the aggressive powers—Babylon and Egypt—contending for supremacy. Jehoiakim first fell under the domination of Egypt and paid a heavy tribute. Thus began the shadow of vassalage, which plunged the nation into a course of subjection that never ended.

Unhappy kings, without ability to resist mighty neighbors, led their people into misery and despair. Through the long agony of a quarter century, Jeremiah stood alone, discerning clearly what lay ahead and trying to avert the tragedy of a dying kingdom.

As opinion hardened around the Anathothite, he lost none of his warmth of heart. Nor did he falter in the face of fierce opposition to point out the only wise course the nation could take as the storm approached. His wonderful breadth of sympathy grieved for the suffering he knew would surely come.

But only the perverted logic of hysteria, the insatiable desire to reach for futile panaceas greeted his efforts. There is only one way to meet the challenges of life, and the prophet made it clear that no dependence on the arms of man, no matter how strong, is sufficient in a crisis.

"Thus says the Lord: 'Let not the wise man glory in his wisdom, let not the mighty man glory in his might, let not the rich man glory in his riches; but let him who glories glory in this, that he understands and knows me, that I am the Lord who practice steadfast love, justice, and righteousness in the earth; for in these things I delight' " (9:23, 24).

How did his people respond?

They plunged deeper into the idolatry of other nations. In chapter 10 Jeremiah tells how they built images to other gods, then plated them with silver from Tarshish and gold from Uphaz, thought by some to be Ophir and so named in the New English Bible.

Gold does not create happiness but only an enjoyable kind of bewitching misery.

Said a dying man to his nephew, "I leave you my fortune, but never forget that wealth does not bring happiness."

"I know it," answered the young man, "but I'll be glad to get it so as to choose the misery which is most agreeable to me."

In this vein Jeremiah advised the rich man not to glory in his riches. Nor should his countrymen spread their gold on idols. Neither would save anyone in the days of trouble ahead.

A newspaper held a contest for the best definition of money. The prize submission ran like this: "Money is a universal provider for everything but happiness, and a passport everywhere but to heaven."

Apparently in Jeremiah's day gold was being used to beautify idols and glorify oneself. But all would perish, predicted the prophet, and time proved him right.

One does not fix the plumbing by blowing up the kitchen sink. Neither did God cast off His backsliding people without doing everything possible to mend their faulty pipelines of faith.

One of the inescapable facts of history to notice in this connection is the unfailing moral declension that invariably attends the passage of time. There often occur periods of rejuvenation or strong revivals—as with Josiah—but the general trend returns and the decline continues.

There may be material prosperity, rapid growth in formal religion, cultural and intellectual advance, but never has a country or a people been able to withstand the erosive effect of time upon its moral structure. This is a fact of history every church, all society, each person, should face and then candidly appraise itself or himself accordingly.

The corrosive tendency of time overtook Israel with disastrous results, and Jeremiah tried valiantly to check or delay the downward trend. Came then the final day of rude awakening to lost opportunity, neglected privileges, and perverted ways. "Then the cities of Judah and the inhabitants of Jerusalem will go and cry to the gods to whom they burn incense, but they cannot save them in the time of their trouble" (11:12).

So spoke the great man who never for fear or favor withheld what God told him to reveal. All Heaven-appointed men have certain things in common. For instance, what F. B. Meyer said of D. L. Moody also could hold true of Jeremiah:

"He was preeminently a strong man: nothing short of indomitable resolution and willpower could have conducted the uncultured, uneducated lad from the old shanty in Chicago to the

Opera House in London, where royalty waited on his words—
rugged, terse, direct, and sharp as a two-edged sword: for as the
man was, so he spoke. . . . The charm of his character was his
thorough naturalness. . . . At the same time he was absolutely
simple and humble; . . . and . . . [he] determined that people
should rest on the Word of God, to which he was ever pointing
them. He therefore encased himself in the hard shell of an apparently rugged manner."

The difference, of course, between Moody and Jeremiah lay in
the way people received them. Moody spared no words in calling
for repentance, and the masses responded. Jeremiah's call met the
bitterest resistance because men from the king down were ir-
recoverably bent on evil. The Biblical preacher sounded, in principle, the very same call by which the American evangelist began
his sermon "Where Art Thou?"

As soon as the news of man's fall reached heaven, God came
straight down to seek out the lost one. As He walked through the
Garden in the cool of the day He called, "Adam! Adam! *Where art
thou?*" It was the voice of grace, of mercy, and of love. Adam, the
transgressor, ought to have taken the seeker's place. He had fallen,
and he ought to have gone up and down Eden crying, "My God!
my God! where art Thou?" But God left heaven to seek through the
dark world for the rebel who had fallen—not to hurl him from the
face of the earth but to plan for him a way of escape from the
misery of his sin. And He found him—where? Hiding from his
Creator among the bushes of the Garden.

Paralleling the same vigorous style of speech that Jeremiah
employed, Moody went on to say:

"When I was in England in 1867, a merchant came over from
Dublin and talked with a businessman in London. As I happened
to look in, he introduced me to the man from Dublin. Alluding to
me, the latter said to the former, 'Is this young man an O O?' Said
the London man, 'What do you mean by O O?' Replied the Dublin
man, 'Is he Out-and-Out for Christ?' I tell you it burned down into
my soul. It means a good deal to be O O for Christ; but that is what
all Christians ought to be. Their influence would be felt on the
world very soon if men who are on the Lord's side would come out
and take a stand, lifting up their voices in season and out of

season. As I have said, there are a great many in the church who once made a profession, and that is about all you hear of them; when they die you have to go and hunt up some church records to know whether they were Christians or not. God will not do that. I have an idea that when Daniel died, all the men in Babylon knew whom he served. There was no need for them to hunt up old books. His life told his story. What we want are men with a little courage to stand up for Christ. When Christianity wakes up, and every child that belongs to the Lord is willing to speak for Him, is willing to work for Him, and if need be, willing to die for Him, then Christianity will advance, and we shall see the work of the Lord prosper."

Jeremiah strove to accomplish the same thing in Judah. His message of doom warned men of the dire consequences if they refused to repent and reform their lives.

With this objective he returned occasionally to his home at Anathoth. He told the townsmen they could not have both worlds and expect to win God's favor. "Stop this headlong plunge into Baalism, cease compromising, repent, or perish!" he cried.

Like a sheep he went to the slaughter, innocently telling Anathoth to mend its ways. But evil designs were in the making. "I did not know," he says, "that they were hatching plots against me" (11:19, NEB).

They wanted to cut down the prophesying tree. "Let us destroy him, . . . so that his very name shall be forgotten" (11:19, NEB).

A crowd of citizens, worked up into a panic of rage over his cutting revelations, confronted him. "Prophesy no more in the name of the Lord," they roared, "or we will kill you!" (11:21, NEB).

The hate reflecting on their faces shocked Jeremiah.

The gloves were now off and both sides of a simmering controversy (God, Jeremiah, and secret admirers on one side) waded in, but not as yet for a complete knockout.

This incident precipitated a mania to silence the prophet, even if it meant taking his life. From Anathoth the-hate-Jeremiah frenzy spread rapidly through the land.

Jeremiah went on keeping his charge, believing God would

repay the good and the evil. It is far better, he advised men, to pour the golden treasures of Uphaz into good deeds rather than on the vain works of their own hands. Through pleasant and cloudy weather he set the pace that all men should emulate:

"O Lord of Hosts who art a righteous judge,
      testing the heart and mind,
      I have committed my cause to thee" (11:20, NEB).

Anyone at Anathoth could have felt all the hardness of heart and bitter hatred melt out of his soul if he had understood Jeremiah's gentle concern and God's benign purpose.

We can almost see Jeremiah searching for words as the irate townspeople confront him. It was an occasion when a hard-pressed person could have made a symbolic circle with his arms. Then an extraordinary man such as Jeremiah—tall and brave, straight as an arrow, his sympathetic eyes searching the motley crowd—would have said, "God wants to enclose all of us in His great arms of love."

It would have been a beautiful scene of sweet reconciliation had the people only responded to appeals like this.

Chapter 10

THE WINE CUPS OF RECHAB *

The Essence of Life: "Strike! We have nothing to lose but our chains," cried the angry young dissident.

"But," replied the father, "there's also your conscience. Which is no trivial matter."

When Jeremiah, having been run out of his hometown, returned to Jerusalem, he found the superstitious breed proliferating more than ever. A wave of fascination with Babylonian astrology and Canaanite sex perversion had swept through the city.

A cool relentlessness in seeking the new freedoms decreased Jeremiah's already fading hope for any reforms. "We have broken the old chains," enthused the occultists. "Now we have the best of both worlds." But a demonic subculture lay beneath the surface, ready to catch the whole nation in a horrible disaster, and Jeremiah knew it.

It reminds one of the occult craze sweeping the world today. In its cover article of June 19, 1972, *Time* magazine notes: "A wave of fascination with the occult is noticeable throughout the country."

The phenomenon ranges from astrology through raw Satan worship to ceremonial orgies such as this: "When the moon is full, a group of college-educated people gather in a house in a middle-class neighborhood, remove their clothes, and whirl through the double spiral of a witches' dance."

The scene in Jerusalem was tinged with such foul worship, but the heart of the new movement toward the religious left was more respectable; it involved elements of compromise and accommodation that disarmed the complacent center. Of course, over on the far right a fanatical wing held tenaciously to a Temple cult of extreme bigotry: "This is the Temple of God; all the armies in the world could never harm it."

Against all of this, Jeremiah leveled his arrows. Chapter 26

---

*This chapter based on Jeremiah 26; 35; 22:1-19.

starts this way: "In the beginning of the reign of Jehoiakim the son of Josiah, king of Judah, this word came from the Lord, 'Thus says the Lord: Stand in the court of the Lord's house, and speak; . . . do not hold back a word' " (26:1, 2).

According to this scenario, the prophet, after a night of soul-searching and divine consultation, goes to the Temple court. The year is 605 BC. Jeremiah, now around age forty, has been for years standing up to be counted while the brickbats were flying. He has solid credentials as a prophet in the eyes of many but is regarded a dangerous troublemaker by a group of diehard leaders.

As an excited crowd gathers, two priests follow a common man from the streets toward the center of interest. We shall give these priests the names of Jeruiah and Zadok, though actually the names are imaginary.

"What's going on?" they ask a man on the street.

"The prophet is back! He's over there, getting ready to speak."

"Oh," groans Jeruiah, "he's here again. I heard they ran him out of Anathoth."

Zadok does not share the-hate-Jeremiah mood gripping most of his fellow priests. So the two speak briefly about their differing views while walking toward the Temple court.

"Remember the good old days of King Josiah?" queries Zadok. "He was a puritan—and don't forget that Jeremiah stood with him. Those were the days when the country prospered."

"Well," drawls Jeruiah, "it was narrow puritan severity. The chains were too heavy for the people, and this Jeremiah wants to keep us bound and fettered."

"Narrow puritan severity," repeats Zadok reflectively. "That's just a convenient term of the freewheelers for a decent, scrupulous life, denying self, caring for others, and being careful about how one takes his religion."

Jeruiah becomes a little impatient at his straitlaced companion. "That's what you think. Jehoiakim is a liberal, practical man of the world. With the Babylonians getting closer, his type is better suited to our needs. Besides, people don't like to be straitjacketed all the time."

Zadok disagrees. "Our strength is in the old faith. The nation always prospered when we lived it."

"Come, now," replies Jeruiah, "there are beauty and virtue in other religions. We might learn something. Take the best they have and put it with the best we have."

By then the two priests have arrived at the place where Jeremiah is pleading with the people to repent. His mere presence draws a crowd, for he had been the dominant influence in Judah during the years of Josiah's reign, a time some now remember with intense nostalgia.

Jeremiah tells the crowd that the curse of God will be lifted and the city spared if they obey the Lord and listen to His prophets. But no, this won't happen, he goes on to say. He can see no signs of repentance; so the city and the Temple are doomed.

A priest cries out, "Traitor! It isn't true!"

A wild frenzy seizes priests and people. They lay hands on Jeremiah and jostle him to the gate where officers of the royal court, aroused by the commotion, have assembled for a hearing.

Priests and Temple prophets demand quick action. "Condemn this fellow to death. He has prophesied against this city: you have heard it with your own ears" (26:11, NEB).

Jeremiah's defense sounds reasonable. "The Lord sent me," he begins, "to prophesy against this house and this city all that you have heard. If you now mend your ways and your doings and obey the Lord your God, then he may relent and revoke the disaster with which he has threatened you" (26:12, 13, NEB).

The officers are impressed; the people, too, begin to think differently of the man they were ready to kill a short time before. One of the elders arises and points out how King Hezekiah, whose name is venerated, repented at a similar rebuke by Micah. Thus the tide turns in the prophet's favor.

But the priests, their professional pride stung, and the Temple prophets, envious of Jeremiah's superior gift of speech, are still deeply prejudiced, only awaiting another chance to strike back.

"Maybe that close call will silence him," remarks Jeruiah as he and his fellow priests walk away.

"Not that man," observes Zadok. "He's as enduring as the building stones we get from the quarries at Anathoth."

"Better be careful, friend—he's a marked man. Don't get caught on his side."

Having escaped his enemies, the Anathothite turned to the Rechabites—still "in the days of Jehoiakim" (35:1 |chronology now takes us from chapter 26 to chapter 35|).

These descendants of Rechab, now incorporated into the Jewish nation, lived a nomadic life and adhered to a solemn vow of abstinence from wine—a vow Jonadab, the son of their founder, had enjoined upon them. Jeremiah brought a group of the Rechabites to the Temple and placed pitchers of wine with drinking cups before them.

"Drink the wine," invited the prophet, knowing full well what their response would be.

"We will drink no wine," they said.

The lesson was clear: If these nomads were so faithful in keeping the vow enjoined upon them by their ancestor, should not Israel be equally determined to obey God?

Thus the wine cups of Rechab remained empty, and Jeremiah made a telling point for the whole nation to ponder. In fact, they have stood ever since as a reminder to millions that obedience in all the details of life wins Heaven's approval and favor.

Jehoiakim, the king, did not take kindly to the prophet's admonitions. Avarice, cruelty, oppression, violence, and false worship marked his troubled reign. The usually accepted sequence now goes back to chapter 22 where Jeremiah fearlessly denounces the king, who, without adequate resources, had plunged into a mad imitation of Babylon's magnificent building program. It seemed to be an unreasoning attempt to copy the luxury of the world by using forced labor and unjust practices. Cried the prophet, "Shame on the man who builds his house by unjust means and completes its roof-chambers by fraud, making his countrymen work without payment, giving them no wage for their labour!" (22:13, NEB).

The prophet, without counting the cost, fearlessly conveyed to the astonished king just what God commanded him to say: "Therefore these are the words of the Lord concerning Jehoiakim son of Josiah, king of Judah: . . . He shall be buried like a dead ass" (22:18, 19, NEB).

Actually, times have not changed much since Jeremiah told Jehoiakim that obedience is the only way to peace and happiness.

Chapter 11

WINE OF WRATH *

The Essence of Life: "And this is eternal life, that they know thee the only true God, and Jesus Christ whom thou hast sent" (John 17:3).

"For twenty-three years, . . . I have spoken persistently to you, but you have not listened" (25:3).

That is what Jeremiah told his countrymen. But since no one seemed to pay attention to what the prophet said, something drastic was needed—when easy teaching is refused, learning has to come the hard way. And 25:1 sets the stage for such a learning experience: "That was the first year of Nebuchadnezzar king of Babylon."

Jeremiah announced the decision of God: Babylonian conquest would provide special medication for healing the diseased mind and heart of a nation. The response of his hearers, totally unable to tolerate any intimation of the sort, seemed downright hysterical, and they replied with vitriol aimed directly at God's spokesman.

They claimed that these endlessly repeated warnings would turn out to be as phony as what was then the equivalent of a three-dollar bill. The popular wisdom of the day, as in Noah's time, rejected the facts of faith and instead tried to put together a system empty of the true religion, yet not wholly pagan in all its forms. One could think of it as trying to pull a chariot with zebras.

I saw something of that sort in the city of Calcutta a few years ago. A wealthy resident drove a fine carriage hitched to two zebras. But the dumb creatures at a critical moment one day decided to end the whole experiment by yielding to a stubborn instinct, and the city streets saw the excitement of wild runaways.

The opposition that voiced bitter resistance in Jerusalem would soon see the results of their blind logic. Jeremiah warned

---

*This chapter based on Jeremiah 25; 18-20.

that they, as well as other nations (some twenty are cited), would be harnessed and made to drink of Babylon's wrath.

"Thus the Lord, the God of Israel, said to me: 'Take from my hand this cup of the wine of wrath, and make all the nations to whom I send you drink it. They shall drink and stagger and be crazed because of the sword which I am sending among them' " (25:15, 16).

It is interesting and revealing that God did not tell Jeremiah to go out on the desert and start a new church. Heaven had a plan to straighten out the one He once established. The prophet did not strike in blind desperation when men turned against him—he waited, prayed, and trusted, all the while faithfully speaking the revelations of God.

Judah would become a desolation at the hands of Babylonian warlords and be in bondage for seventy years. After that, Babylon itself, having fulfilled its appointed place in God's purpose, would be destroyed, but with one striking difference. To its appointed desolation is added a significant word, well attested by history: "I will punish . . . that nation, . . . making the land an *everlasting* waste" (25:12).

The prophet goes on to forecast the final judgment upon the nations of the world—put in here to emphasize the ultimate sovereignty of God over the entire earth right down to the end of time. In that day judgment is to "extend from one end of the earth to the other" (25:33).

"Thus says the Lord of hosts:
Behold, evil is going forth
    from nation to nation,
and a great tempest is stirring
    from the farthest parts of the earth!" (25:32).

The prophet is now sent to the potter's house (chapter 18), where he sees the clay spoiled, then reworked to the potter's liking. God informs him of the purpose: "Like the clay in the potter's hand, so are you in my hand, O house of Israel" (18:6). The message: "Repent, change your evil ways, and everything will be different." But this doesn't happen. "We will follow our own plans" (18:12), the people determine. Their delusions increase and tempers rise:

"Then they said, 'Come, let us make plots against Jeremiah, for the law shall not perish from the priest, nor counsel from the wise, nor the word from the prophet. Come, let us smite him with the tongue, and let us not heed any of his words' " (18:18).

Nothing now remained but some sharp jolts to nudge them out of the track they were beating around their self-imposed slavery.

A captive eagle, tied by a chain to a post, walked around it until a deep circle was worn in the ground. After several years the owner removed the chain, but the eagle kept on making his usual circle. The bird finally claimed his freedom only when someone pushed him from the beaten track.

It takes a push—sometimes a hard one—to get men out of the rut they cut for themselves. God tried it by the comparatively mild method of the prophet's warning voice. Finally extreme measures became necessary when they refused to listen.

God did not want to punish His recalcitrant people, but they left Him no other option. He will not remain silent while confused men deliberately plunge His church headlong into the abyss. So Jeremiah is instructed to buy an earthen flask, which he breaks before the elders with the warning, " 'Thus says the Lord of hosts: So will I break this people and this city, . . . because they have stiffened their neck, refusing to hear my words' " (19:11-15).

Chapter 20 now follows in consecutive order. Pashhur the priest and chief officer arrested the prophet, put him to public torture in painful stocks, thus exhibiting him to the mockery of enemies and the distress of friends.

Suffering humiliation and intense pain, the prophet informs the haughty officer of a change in his name. Instead of Pashhur, he is to be called Terror, for he will look on in terror while those he holds dear are put to the sword before he himself is led captive to Babylon.

Jeremiah is soon released, but haunting fears assail him and, being human, he yields to a sense of frustration. His lifework seems a failure, and he complains bitterly as the ghostly fingers of despair close upon him. "I have become a laughingstock all the day; everyone mocks me" (20:7). Even friends and sympathizers seem to have gone into hiding.

Finally his sensitive spirit can take no more. "I will not mention him, or speak any more in his name," he vows (20:9).

But he cannot remain silent. A fire burns in his bones, he says, even as he hears some of his former friends crying, "Denounce him! Let us denounce him!" Watching every step he takes, they wait for him to fall. "Then," they say, "we can . . . take our revenge on him" (20:10).

The prophet is determined to disappoint these peddlers of deceit and malice. "They will not succeed," he declares with grim resolution (20:11).

The treachery, the hate, the ridicule, however, caught him off guard at times. "Cursed be the day on which I was born!" he cried (20:14). "Why did I come forth from the womb to see toil and sorrow, and spend my days in shame?" (20:18).

Martin Luther, like Jeremiah and most of us, also had his sticky days. He wrote, "At one time I was sorely vexed and tried by my own sinfulness, by the wickedness of the world, and by the dangers which beset the Church. One morning I saw my wife dressed in mourning. Surprised, I asked her who had died. She replied: 'Do you not know? God in Heaven is dead.'

"I said to her: 'How can you talk such nonsense, Katie? How can God die? He is immortal, and will live through all eternity.'

" 'Is that really true?' she asked.

" 'Of course,' I said, still not perceiving what she was aiming at; 'how can you doubt it? As surely as there is a God in Heaven, so sure is it that He can never die.'

" 'And yet,' she said, 'though you do not doubt that, you are still so hopeless and discouraged.'

"Then I observed what a wise woman my wife was, and mastered my sadness" (J. B. McClure, *Pearls From Many Seas*, p. 221).

Jeremiah, too, fought his way out of the quicksands of despair. Along with sweet appeals of God's mercy and readiness to forgive, he sang the songs of praise and confidence. In the midst of his struggle with discouragement he recognized the assurance every downhearted man can find in God's boundless mercy.

> "Sing to the Lord;
>   praise the Lord!
> For he has delivered the life of the needy

from the hand of evildoers" (20:13).

Jeremiah overcame despair because he trusted God when the gentle streams turned to raging rivers. "O Lord of Hosts, thou dost test the righteous and search the depths of the heart" (20:12, NEB).

Why did he have the backup, the powerful reserves, to meet the bitter tests of life? He reveals the secret: "To thee have I committed my cause" (20:12).

Here is complete commitment, total involvement. This means perseverance: continually pressing on when people and events conspire against us. Anything else would have been mockery to Jeremiah.

"Perseverance, dear my lord,
Keeps honour bright; to have done is to hang
Quite out of fashion, like a rusty mail
In monumental mockery."
                    —Shakespeare, *Troilus and Cressida*, Act III, Scene III

Chapter 12

THUNDER OVER JERUSALEM*

The Essence of Life:
"Nor love thy life, nor hate; but what thou livst,
Live well; how long or short permit to Heav'n"
—Milton, *Paradise Lost*

The fate of Jerusalem hung in the balance. Every effort—and there were many—to induce repentance only ended in rejection. The prophet, imprisoned or otherwise severely proscribed, received a command to devise another way to be heard. So we now have the episode of the prophet, the scroll, and the stubborn king.

Baruch, Jeremiah's gifted and devoted secretary, writes the message God gives the prophet, with the sole purpose of saving a nation from the doom she is bringing upon herself. "Perhaps the house of Judah will be warned of the calamity that I am planning to bring on them, and every man will abandon his evil course; then I will forgive their wrongdoing and their sin" (36:3, NEB).

Favorable results appeared very unlikely. This alone would have discouraged most realists, but Jeremiah never measured his work in the popularity arena. He persevered in telling the people the truth they did not want to hear.

Maybe Jeremiah watched the honeybee and thought about his own work. If so, he would have seen one little bee flying thousands of miles carrying tiny amounts of the sweet nectar. But during its working year the little droplets added up to a spoonful. And the combined hive of diligent, persistent creatures gathered no less than one hundred pounds.

The prophet worked on the principle that a man must do his job regardless of the difficulties or the obstacles encountered. It was like the words Joaquin Miller wrote in *Columbus:*

*This chapter based on Jeremiah 36:1-4; 45; 36:5-32; 12. 2 Kings 24:1-4.

> " 'Brave Adm'r'l, say but one good word:
> What shall we do when hope is gone?'
> The words leapt like a leaping sword:
> 'Sail on! sail on! sail on! and on!' "

Jeremiah kept going on. When he denounced entangling alliances with Egypt and urged a more friendly attitude toward the rising power of Babylon, his countrymen condemned him. But he did not stop telling them about the disasters that lay ahead.

Many, unknown to the hard-pressed prophet, quietly repeated his words in their homes. Children grew up respecting the lone, brave prophet from Anathoth. Among these were youths such as Daniel and his companions. No doubt they were well acquainted with Jeremiah's work when the Babylonians carried them away into captivity.

Baruch, a young man of culture, social standing, and ambition, probably felt it a privilege to be associated with a great prophet. "What a golden opportunity!" he might have exclaimed.

The aspiring young secretary, however, met with some disappointments that dazed but did not stop him. After dictating the scroll, Jeremiah in chapter 45 (which in order of time follows the first part of chapter 36) gave a short utterance to his assistant. Chapter 45 only has five verses, but they tell much about Baruch.

"O Baruch!"

There is a mild rebuke in Jeremiah's voice as he warns his disciple of a bitter root in his soul that might get out of control and destroy him. His hope of an exciting life and a share in the honor one could expect a great prophet to receive had been shattered.

So Baruch complained, " 'Woe is me!' "

Instead of the dreams he fondly cherished, he had endured the hardships and reproaches that fell upon his teacher. Now he has been asked to take the scroll and read it to the nobles at the palace. Jeremiah, of course, could not do it, for he was still under a nominal house arrest. They both knew it would be dangerous.

"The Lord has added sorrow to my pain. I am weary with my groaning, and I find no rest" (45:3), he laments.

Jeremiah has a message from God for him: The great thing of glory and praise—His church, called Israel—that He built up will now be broken down. Nothing will avert the disaster.

Perhaps Baruch, the ambitious son of Neriah, thought that after reading the scroll he could intercede at court and bring about a reconciliation. Thus he would not only save the nation but his beloved master as well and perform a great service on his own. He could see that Jeremiah's blunt, direct ways often antagonized people. He now had a chance to apply soothing oil, which of course would add luster to his name and actually benefit the prophet.

"Do you seek great things for yourself?" asks the discerning prophet, instructed by God Himself to put the question. "Seek them not" (45:5).

The nation, hopelessly corrupt, has reached the point of no return. It is useless to think of a change. Only hard bondage will restore the pristine beauty of His heritage. So Baruch, showing the intrinsic integrity and loyalty of his soul, goes with the scroll to the people, then to the princes who listen with mixed emotions. Some are for executing the prophet forthwith, but several stand in his defense. All this takes us back to chapter 36.

To the credit of the princes, it must be said that they acted to protect the two men who were now in imminent danger of their lives. "Go and hide," said they, "you and Jeremiah, and let no one know where you are" (36:19).

When the princes presented the scroll to the king, he erupted. "Burn it!" he roared. Three of the princes urged him to desist, but he refused, and the message from God went up in smoke.

At this time Jeremiah again yields to the sensitivity of his tender feelings. Chapter 12 gives his own reactions and a revealed sense of divine sorrow for outrageous conduct. While the prophet and his disciple wait in silence for God to act, their thoughts turn to a philosophy of life.

"Why does the way of the wicked prosper? Why do all who are treacherous thrive?" (12:1).

The question has been asked by a million others. And probably the two men discussed the matter over and over as they sat in lonely hiding. It seems difficult to harmonize all the facts of human experience, but God gives Jeremiah some light on the vexing questions of life.

"If you have raced with men on foot,

> and they have wearied you,
> how will you compete with horses?
> And if in a safe land you fall down,
> how will you do in the jungle of
> the Jordan?" (12:5).

"If we cannot endure the lesser troubles of life, how can we withstand the terrible tribulations that will yet come upon us? And finally, if we fail to meet the situations of the present day with faith and trust, how will we be able to stand the almost unendurable hardships and almost overmastering delusions that will come upon us during the 'time of trouble'?" (*The Seventh-day Adventist Bible Commentary*, Vol. 4, p. 408).

Something else bothered Jeremiah, but he met it without difficulty. His family came to him with flattering words—perhaps instigated by the prophet's opponents. One can almost hear them say, "Moderate your tone. With your ability and fame you could become the most popular man in the country. Even the king might be glad to shower favors upon you if you'd just play along with the mood of the country."

God told Jeremiah that his brothers' suggestions amounted to treachery: "Believe them not, though they speak fair words to you" (12:6).

Too late for that kind of talk! With the die already cast, Nebuchadnezzar's armies advanced. Thunder broke over Jerusalem. The irresistible tempest from the east overwhelmed that part of the world, swallowing up Jerusalem in the implacable flood of Babylonian conquest.

Jehoiakim, put in chains, was led captive to Babylon, to be later restored after his apparent submission. But the headstrong king learned nothing from his tribulations or the warnings of Jeremiah. Three years later he rebelled. Nebuchadnezzar let the surrounding tribes ravage the land; at length the mercurial, cruel king was killed and buried, "with the burial of an ass . . . beyond the gates of Jerusalem" (22:19).

Beyond the thunder and tempest lay bright days of hope and promise. God uses pain to serve a benign purpose. Life is sweetened by this unfailing assurance. To his troubled land, Jeremiah conveyed God's promise: "After I have plucked them up, I will again have compassion on them, and I will bring them again each to his heritage and each to his land" (12:15).

So let it thunder over Jerusalem. God lives above the storm, working out a beneficent purpose. That is precisely what Jeremiah tried to tell his people.

God is telling men the same today. Amid all the confusion and distress, the evil and despair, Heaven is working out a plan for their eternal good. There are mysteries one cannot understand, thorns that puncture tender flesh, briers to tear the clothes; but the flowers of God await His own good time and purpose.

Chapter 13

100 DAYS OF THE YOUNG LION*

The Essence of Life: "Entire surrender of your ways, which seem so very wise, and taking Christ's ways, is the secret of perfect rest" (Ellen White, *My Life Today*, p. 176).

"The king is dead. Long live the king!"

But Jehoiachin, the new king, did not last long on the throne—in fact, only three months and ten days. At eighteen he was already old in sin. The Bible simply says, "He did what was evil in the sight of the Lord" (2 Kings 24:9). Yet he appears to have been a remarkable man who packed some dramatic action into his one hundred days on the throne.

A pro-Egyptian party, antagonistic to Jeremiah and opposed to Babylon, still prevailed at court. There is more behind the Bible scene than one reads on the surface.

Ezekiel, who went to Babylon among the captives and apparently held rather sympathetic feelings toward the young king, gives what is thought to be a colorful sidelight on Jehoiachin:

"He prowled among the lions
and acted like a young lion.
He learnt to tear his prey,
he devoured men;
he broke down their palaces, laid their cities in ruins.
The land and all that was in it
was aghast at the noise of his roaring.
From the provinces all round
the nations raised the hue and cry;
they cast their net over him
and he was caught in their pit.
With hooks they drew him into a cage
and brought him to the king of Babylon,

*This chapter based on Jeremiah 22:20-30; 13; 23. 2 Kings 24:8-16.

who flung him into prison,
that his voice might never again be heard
on the mountains of Israel" (Ezekiel 19:6-9, NEB).

With this hyperbole and other evidence in mind, let us conjure up some happenings that could have taken place in Jerusalem.

No sooner has Jehoiachin mounted the throne than an escaped Jewish captive from Babylon rides into Jerusalem with disturbing news.

"A large Babylonian army is marching this way, and Nebuchadnezzar himself is in charge," announces the messenger, who has ridden hard to warn his threatened country. A hasty consultation among the leaders estimates the Babylonians will reach Judah in about two or three months.

A spirited debate follows. Some of the counselors favor sending a delegation to sue for the best terms possible. But the majority, encouraged by Nehushta, the energetic queen mother, favor resistance.

Though recognized as risky, this was adopted because of a belief in Egyptian intervention. Nehushta, an ardent admirer—and imitator—of Egyptian fads and fashions, always wanted her son to look in that direction. The ways of the Egyptians appealed to her pride and vanity more than the unsophisticated faith of the Hebrews. Her influence in this respect was passed on to her children and court attendants. (We are assuming all this, of course.)

Jucal, one of the princes, speaks:

"I consulted Pharaoh's ambassador last week. He indicated that if a crisis arose, help might come from that direction, but naturally he could make no firm commitment."

"Let us send a delegation at once into Egypt to seek help," Elishama, the chief scribe, urges.

"Pharaoh will not let us down," affirms Pashhur, a leader of the pro-Egyptian faction now ascendant at court.

"And in the meantime?" queries Elnathan, one of Jeremiah's sympathizers.

"In the meantime," exclaims the impetuous king, "we will strike!"

To the populace it seems evident that something exciting is

going on in the palace—probably focusing on a call to arms—and news spreads rapidly through Jerusalem. Tantalizingly, a few words furnishing oblique clues are let slip through the chamber doors. Word reaches Jeremiah, who, knowing a power struggle between the pro-Babylonian and pro-Egyptian factions had surfaced at the succession, sends a message of warning to the palace. Elnathan, realizing the extremely critical nature of the coming crisis, reads it to the assembled court.

"He's at it again," Shephatiah, a confirmed opponent of the prophet, sneers. "He ought to be silenced once and for all."

"Not when the country needs the help of everyone," Gemariah replies, seeking to shield Jeremiah, whom he respects. "A lot of people are afraid that he could be right."

"Leave him alone for now," demands the king. "Let's get down to the business of dealing with our enemies."

Many of the leaders have long envisioned a Judaic-Egyptian axis, and now seems the time to put it into operation. A plan evolves to subdue all the neighboring countries in order to deprive the Babylonians of their help. But first, offerings must be made at various altars, beginning at the Temple; care is taken not to overlook the Egyptian shrine in the ambassador's house. Nehushta makes herself conspicuous in this act of diplomacy.

"I think it's important," she once told a wavering nobleman, confused by the trend toward mysticism, "to be flexible. I make it a point to keep up with the popular trends—especially those that reflect Egyptian sophistication."

Now she is swept up in the wave of enthusiasm that favors war. Being the personal epicenter of Egyptian style and mysticism (she sometimes spent hours studying fashion reports), the queen mother feels the euphoria suddenly inspiring Judah.

In an incredibly short time military preparations are completed, and the young king, like a roaring lion, strikes lightning blows at the surrounding petty states. Cities are laid waste, palaces razed, and hostile armies scattered. "A new Joshua!" enthuse the warriors of Judah. The expectation of victory over the Chaldeans rises to a fever pitch—with the assistance of a powerful Egyptian army in mind, of course.

But a big cloud clutters the blue skies. Jeremiah's voice sounds nothing but doom. A disturbing message in the name of God comes to the palace. It sends Nehushta's hot temper into a towering rage and dampens the spirits of the conquering king.

He will fall into the hand of Nebuchadnezzar, Jeremiah informs him. "As I live, says the Lord, . . . I will hurl you and the mother who bore you into another country, where you were not born, and there you shall die" (22:24-26).

Taking a jar, the prophet appeared before the leaders, loath to hear him, and announced, "Every jar shall be filled with wine."

They answered haughtily, "Do we not indeed know that every jar will be filled with wine?" (13:12).

"Of course you know, but what you don't want to hear is the thing that comes next," Jeremiah explained. "They will be filled with drunkenness and dashed about like fragile jars." Why all of this?

> "Can the Nubian change his skin,
>   or the leopard its spots?
> And you? Can you do good,
>   you who are schooled in evil?"
>   (13:23, NEB).

Thus Jeremiah put his finger on the trouble. They had been taught the wrong things from childhood up. Today we would say it's the visual intake: wrong television, polluted reading, permissiveness, sex freedom, luxury. And where lies the responsibility for Israel's despair? While the enemy advances, who is confusing the people?

"Woe to the shepherds |guardians, leaders, teachers, pastors, parents| who destroy and scatter the sheep of my pasture!" (23:1).

Jeremiah has news from God for those incense-burning, Baal-infatuated leaders who neglect their duty and teach falsehood:

"I will attend to you" (23:2).

Suddenly the mighty armies of Babylon appear, and Jerusalem beholds a terrifying sight.

Where are the Egyptians?

Somebody's faulty arithmetic did not add up right. Instead of thousands of Egyptian troops, the number came to zero. The grave miscalculation, the looking toward Egypt instead of Jeremiah's God, amounted to a catastrophic tactical blunder.

Jerusalem surrendered with scarcely a fight. Resistance seemed futile. The royal family marched out of the city, and along with the cream of the land, they were taken captive to Babylon.

But chapter 23, the cover page of these events, also brings out a sublime purpose: a final parting of the clouds, and azure skies breaking through the heavy overcast. Here we see a new Jeremiah, the gentle purpose, the color and joy of a fresh landscape following the spring storms.

"Then I will gather the remnant of my flock out of all the countries where I have driven them, and I will bring them back to their fold, and they shall be fruitful and multiply. I will set shepherds over them who will care for them, and they shall fear no more, nor be dismayed, neither shall any be missing, says the Lord" (23:3, 4).

The misery and despair of life will lead at last to glowing days of hopes realized and promises verified. Every man who patiently endures the corrective process will learn the pleasant melodies of the spheres as God's grand purpose turns pain to everlasting joy.

Jehoiachin, the restless young lion, roars no more; but he too finds peace. This, however, is thirty-seven years later and another chapter.

The hills will ring with joyful sounds. Jeremiah, the messenger of doomsday, intersperses his announcements with sunbursts of glory. The Righteous Branch—the long-awaited Redeemer—will come at last. Life will be full and overflowing. Transports of joy attend the quest of each aspiring heart. Indeed, the Lord is our righteousness (see 23:5, 6).

Jeremiah said it. God confirms it. Every man can have it.

Chapter 14

A CITY UPON HER LITTLE HILL*

The Essence of Life:
> "And you, Jacob my servant, have no fear;
>> despair not, O Israel, says the Lord.
>
> For I will bring you back safe. . . .
>> Be at rest once more,
>> prosperous and unafraid.
>
> For I am with you and will save you, says the Lord"
>> (30:10, 11, NEB).

Jeremiah never failed to hold out hope, nor did predictions about the triumph of Judah's enemy diminish his patriotism. He was in tune with the melody that would have brought peace to the troubled nation. It became the cornerstone of his basic policy.

Instead of undermining his country's security, as opponents charged, he sought to save it by advocating a policy of coming to terms with reality. Moreover, the prophet acted like a physician: only painful surgery served to heal the patient. Tremble, bleed, forget, and smile—this was how he wanted his people to look on the changing times ahead.

They would learn, no matter what happened, that things could be much worse. I realized this while listening to a sermon comparing love to the gas tank in a car. Most autos could never run without the vital fluid.

"Yes, and the water system too," I said to myself, thinking of the water pump in my car, which gave out that very morning.

Dwelling upon car troubles, my mind took on a trace of self-pity, only to be brought back to sanity by the speaker's telling of a beggar he once saw in Shanghai. The poor fellow, without the use of hands or feet, slid along on his stomach, his head pushing the begging bowl. Little troubles quickly faded as I compared the wretched beggar's condition to all my advantages and blessings.

---

*This chapter based on Jeremiah 24; 29; 30.

Jeremiah strove to get men's minds away from their troubles and diversionary concerns toward the values that really mattered. Difficulties—like sudden spring showers that quickly pass, leaving the world glistening and bright—would make them better men and women. Tough challenges were designed to bring out hidden potentials. The test of Babylonian captivity would be the food that makes faith grow.

In this vein there came to Jeremiah a vision of how disaster is turned to good account. In chapter 24 he sees two baskets of figs: one very good, the other spoiled beyond eating.

"Then the word of the Lord came to me: 'Thus says the Lord, the God of Israel: Like these good figs, so I will regard as good the exiles from Judah, whom I have sent away from this place to the land of the Chaldeans. I will set my eyes upon them for good, and I will bring them back to this land. I will build them up, and not tear them down; I will plant them, and not uproot them. I will give them a heart to know that I am the Lord; and they shall be my people and I will be their God, for they shall return to me with their whole heart' " (24:4-7).

The bad figs represented those who were left in Jerusalem, thereby not subjected to the refining rigors of captivity. It also included those who went into Egypt on their own volition and adopted the ways of that land.

The prophet sent a letter to the dejected captives in Babylon advising them to settle down for a long stay of seventy years. There they would find peace if peace reigned in their minds. But restless spirits rose among them, and out of a troubled atmosphere two false and scandalous self-appointed prophets boldly contradicted Jeremiah's counsel. Their seditious activities and immoral conduct finally caused Nebuchadnezzar to consign them to the flames.

No one can stop people from thinking. But someone can always start them thinking. The prophet from Anathoth did just that—he let his captive people, distressed and confused, know that God doesn't forget anyone, even those who have brought trouble upon themselves. The sun breaks through the clouds and a crystal shaft of light pierces the wet, gloomy earth as the prophet reveals God's gracious purpose:

"For I know the plans I have for you, says the Lord, plans for welfare and not for evil, to give you a future and a hope. Then you will call upon me and come and pray to me, and I will hear you. You will seek me and find me; when you seek me with all your heart, I will be found by you, says the Lord, and I will restore your fortunes and gather you" (29:11-14).

Yet, alas!

The time of Jacob's trouble lies ahead. It came to the captives. It comes to all men sooner or later. At last it will come to the entire world just before the final deliverance.

Trouble indeed is coming to Jacob (God's people): "It is a time of distress for Jacob; yet he shall be saved out of it" (30:7). The point to keep in mind is this: Jacob is going to be saved. Never forget it. Jeremiah drove the fact home with all the conviction of his passionate soul. One is reminded of John Hancock's words as he signed the Declaration of Independence: "There! . . . |King George III| can read that name without spectacles!"

This is just about how Jeremiah emphasized two points in particular. First: Do wrong and suffer the inevitable consequences. Second: He who suffers, yet keeps the faith, can be sure of God's love, guidance, and comfort.

" 'Fear not,' " the prophet is bidden to write to his disconsolate people, despairing of ever seeing happy days again. " 'I am with you to save you, says the Lord' " (30:10, 11).

Everything looks bad. You've made a sorry mess of things. "Your hurt is incurable. . . . There is . . . no medicine |human help, that is| for your wound" (30:12, 13).

Old friends have dropped you. No one seems to understand or care anymore. "All your lovers have forgotten you; they care nothing for you" (30:14).

The roses still bloom, it is true, but thorns seem to be getting bigger and sharper. Here we are—captives in Babylon: slaves or servants unable to extricate ourselves from trouble. What can be done about it? Well, there is much that can be done.

Take, for example, a present-day woman that Brad Ramsey writes about in the *Sunshine Magazine* of July, 1972.

"She was a most pleasant lady in her early forties. Her most attractive features were eyes that held deep pools of patience and a faint smile worn only by those who have conquered.

"For a moment her gaze darted to the open window, and she seemed to drink in the sunlight that spilled between the open curtains.

" 'Well, I love to work in the flowers,' she said. 'I love to just crawl among the flowers and dig in the flower beds, and I love to smell the flowers. Especially the roses! Sometimes I get stuck crawling among the roses, but in spite of the thorns I love the roses!'

"Now, it is not unusual to find a woman who likes to work in the flower garden. But this lady was in a nursing home, and she had been confined to her bed with a baffling and incurable illness for more than seventeen years. She couldn't stand; she could not as much as sit up. The only way she could move about on her own strength was to lie on her stomach and pull herself about with her hands.

"On sunny days the nurses would carry her out to the flower beds, where she would lie on her stomach and dig among the flowers, crawling from one flower bed to the other. 'In spite of the thorns I love the roses!' . . .

"When an adversity comes, I remember the little emaciated body, the big eyes and faint smile, and I hold the adversity up to life and repeat the words, 'In spite of the thorns I love the roses!' "

One gets something like this from Jeremiah—healing and beauty amid the thorns. After citing the troubles of Israel, he writes these words: "I will restore health to you, and your wounds I will heal, says the Lord" (30:17).

Jerusalem will again rise from shambles. "The city shall be rebuilt upon its mound" (30:18).

It's going to be altogether good and supremely joyful (as always happens when God directs men and women).

> "Out of them shall come songs of
> thanksgiving,
> and the voices of those who make
> merry" (30:19).

A gleaming new city of hope and beauty rises from the human wreckage on the little hills of life. Children laugh, men smile, the incurable are healed. "I will multiply them" (30:19), says the Lord.

In place of sorrow, fear, and frustration there will be joy, confidence, and favor. "You shall be my people, and I will be your God" (30:22).

Every cloudy day on earth yields in time to radiant sunshine as God solves our problems for us. Finally Paradise, wonderful beyond words to describe, awaits the tried and proved disciples of Christ, buffeted, scarred, and wounded but magnificently triumphant.

Chapter 15

A TALE OF THE TOLAS*

The Essence of Life:

"I have dearly loved you from of old,
 and still I maintain my unfailing care for you.
 I will build you up again, O virgin Israel" (31:3, 4, NEB).

Chapter 31 is a monument of surpassing beauty on a dramatic landscape of inspiration.

Jehovah is pictured as calling the unhappy exiles home. "The time is coming when I will restore the fortunes of my people," Jeremiah is commanded to write.

"Break into shouts of joy for Jacob's sake, . . . sing out your praises" (31:7, NEB).

The causes are not far to seek: "The Lord has saved his people. . . . See how I bring them, . . . their blind and lame among them, women with child and women in labour" (31:7, 8, NEB).

What a joyful company—coming by the way of cool streams flowing in a blazing desert:

"They come home, weeping as they come,
     but I will comfort them and be their escort.
 I will lead them to flowing streams;
   they shall not stumble, their path will be so smooth.
     For I have become a father to Israel" (31:9, NEB).

The bright scene expands—God's measureless blessings promised to all the faithful as the sorrowful are made glad:

"They shall come with shouts of joy, . . .
  shining with happiness
     at the bounty of the Lord" (31:12, NEB).

Ah—the delightful scenes, the pleasant vistas of a people who have found favor before the Lord! Jeremiah uses the sweetest analogies to describe their blessedness. The prophet of doom

---

*This chapter based on Jeremiah 31; 46; 47. The story of the Tolas is imaginary, although it does no violence to the actual text.

splashes new colors upon landscapes of charm and beauty:
  "They shall become like a watered garden
     and they shall never want again" (31:12, NEB).
  The promise becomes transcendent, exultant, jubilant: "I will
turn their mourning into gladness" (31:13, NEB).
  These were scenes in the future that the prophet saw with great
delight: "I woke and looked about me, and my dream had been
pleasant" (31:26, NEB).
  But now, before those pleasant days of peace and safety, times
of bitter trial must be endured. Verse 15 says, "Hark, lamentation
is heard in Ramah, and bitter weeping, Rachel weeping for her
sons" (NEB). It came to the exiles. Matthew 2:17, 18 borrows these
words from Jeremiah to describe Herod's slaughter of the inno-
cents. Perhaps we can take the liberty of applying it to what could
very well have happened in one of the little huts of the poor exiles
beside the Euphrates River.
  Rachel strives bravely to sustain her family after Tola, her
husband, a wise and faithful man, has been murdered by a brutal
Chaldean overlord for refusing to work on the Sabbath, which he
had always observed with scrupulous care. He had been a leader
among his people, towering above his fellows in appearance,
integrity, and faithfulness. A believer in Jeremiah, he had often
told his family to cherish the prophet's words.
  Now, as Rachel prepares a scanty meal, Shimron, the older
son, enters the humble abode, his face a dark panorama of fury
and resentment. Let us listen as we imagine the scene.
  "What is the matter, my son?" the gentle mother inquires.
  "It's that Chaldean tyrant. Just wait—we're going to get him."
  "What is this you are talking about? You must not hate anyone."
  "Is that so?" replies her troubled son, calmed a shade but not
very much, by her subdued voice. "Well, he shoved me around
again after calling me a dog of a Jew."
  Rachel gently touches her son's shoulder. "Be patient, be patient, my son. Remember the words of Jeremiah's letter that your
father often quoted: 'I have satisfied those who are faint and
hungry.' Let us wait patiently. God surely will keep His word."
  Shimron draws himself up to his full height, and Rachel thinks

how much he looks like her husband.

"Patience!" he blurts out impulsively. "Well, he killed my father, but his turn is coming—and very soon!"

"Tell me, please, what this is all about."

In a low, cautious voice Shimron tells his mother of a plot he and several companions are hatching to kill the ruthless overlord. They have observed that he passes a certain brick wall every night by himself to study the stars. From their hiding place behind the wall they will pounce upon him and then throw his body into the river.

In her first move to head off the dangerous venture, Rachel warns:

"They are almost sure to find the body and suspect foul play."

"Oh, no. Not in our plan. We'll simply strangle him. There will be no marks on his body. It will look like an accident."

"No, my dear son, not that. You must not break the holy law your father died to keep. Besides the Sabbath, it also says, 'Thou shalt not kill.' "

Shimron remains silent, pondering the words his mother spoke. She again quotes the prophet: " 'He who scattered Israel shall gather them again and watch over them as a shepherd watches his flock. For the Lord has ransomed Jacob and redeemed him from a foe too strong for him' " (31:10, 11, NEB).

The very words have a subduing effect upon the impulsive youth. At that moment Miriam, the daughter, steps into the hut with a problem of her own. She is a beautiful girl of extraordinary charm and intelligence, the image of her mother. She had been taught to respect the words of Jeremiah, but of late there have risen certain complications in her life that cause much uncertainty.

To these troubled people, and thousands of other bedraggled exiles like them, some new words—hopeful and encouraging—were coming from the prophet. Chapter 30 closes with a whirlwind of fury falling upon the heads of men. But chapter 31 begins thus: "At that time, says the Lord, I will become God of all the families of Israel, and they shall become my people" (NEB).

Bleeding, despairing, utterly despondent, the once rebellious, backsliding people, denounced by the indignant prophet as the very epitome of spiritual corruption, are now given another character, both pure and beautiful. The figure of an unfaithful wife, a harlot, a degenerate indulging in psychic experiments and the debaucheries of devilism, is changed in Jeremiah's figurative language to a blameless virgin.

Repentant, transformed, and purified in the furnace of affliction, Israel becomes the object of boundless compassion. Now God will not turn her away. He will heal the wounded victim (people have never failed to find it so).

On this basis Rachel always comforted and guided her children. And they never failed to seek her when they needed help. So Miriam pours out her anxiety over something that seems to be the biggest thing in her life at the moment.

"What can I do?" she begs, her countenance displaying a desperate plea for help. "Mother, show me what to do."

"What is it, my daughter?"

"It's Asher; he wants to marry me."

"Tell me about it."

Miriam's lover, it seems, does not share her faith respecting Jeremiah ("He's nothing but a straitlaced faultfinder"), nor does he practice the Jewish religion carefully. A gifted youth in many ways, he has become the favorite of an important family in Babylon who appears ready to bestow on him much favor, which might lead to a highly desirable government position. All this Rachel knows, and some of it she doesn't like.

"What is really bothering you now?" she asks.

"Well, Asher is invited to a big banquet of influential people, and he insists I must go."

"Is it clothes?" asks Rachel. "Maybe we can borrow some."

"No, not that. It's the wine. He insists I have to sip it as a token of respect to the hosts. But I told him that is against my convictions."

Rachel thinks a moment, then poses a question: "What did he say?"

"He became irritated and said something that I didn't like about you and our old-fashioned religious scruples. Finally he told me that I could just touch my lips to the wine cup."

Miriam also has another problem, an ugly frightening one.

"Our overlord sent a message telling me to come and work in his house at the time of the new moon. I'm afraid of him. I don't like the way he comes around and looks at me. Moreover, he's the brute who killed my father. I told Asher about it, and he said his Babylonian friends will certainly protect me. If I'm seen at the banquet, he claims this lord of the exiles will stay as far away from me as he can. Mother, what am I to do?"

"Do the right thing, my child."

"And what is the right thing?"

"Never marry a man who weakens your faith in any way. God always comes first, a husband second—even a husband as good as your father was. As for the other danger, we must trust and pray. God said this to our prophet: 'I will watch over them.' "

Shimron now speaks up. "What that devil of a Chaldean is after will never happen. I'll see to that—if mother consents."

He gives Rachel a meaningful glance. She shakes her head in disapproval.

"What's the meaning of this strange talk?" asks Miriam, mystified by the words she hears.

"A disaster for all of us if it ever happens," replies Rachel. Then she quotes more of Jeremiah's message to the troubled exiles:

" 'But you, Jacob my servant, have no fear,
    despair not, O Israel;
      for I will bring you back safe from afar
        and your offspring from the land
          where they are captives' " (46:27, NEB).

Later in the day Bela, the younger brother, comes home, greatly excited.

"Listen to this!" he cries. "Something big has happened at the palace. It's about Daniel."

"He's our kinsman," says Rachel. "What has happened? Tell us quickly."

"He and his three friends, during a ten-day test, refused to eat the royal meat and drink the king's wine. They drank water and ate vegetables instead."

"Then what?" queries Miriam, calling to mind her own problem with the wine cup.

"Well, listen to this!" shouts Bela almost too excited to speak coherently: "Later, when the king examined them, they were found ten times wiser than all the magicians and astrologers, and now they are favorites at the king's court!"

"Maybe this is the beginning of the favors God promised us through our prophet," observes Rachel thoughtfully.

"I'll call off my murderous plot," vows Shimron as he leaves the hut, profoundly moved by the news about Daniel, his relative.

Before we speculate on the outcome of such a possible incident in Babylon, let us glance very briefly at what Jeremiah actually was doing in Jerusalem at this time.

Chapters 46 and 47 are tentatively believed to fall in order at this point. Pharaoh of Egypt, on whom many in Judah trust, "is but a noise" (46:17, KJV), according to Jeremiah. Nebuchadnezzar will conquer him. Upon the Philistines also will come destruction: "Waters rise up out of the north [Babylon], and shall be an overflowing flood" (47:2, KJV).

The soft promise came to the exiles (and to all hard-pressed people): "Have no fear, says the Lord; for I am with you" (46:28, NEB). Then follows the method, the gracious purpose of divine correction: "Though I punish you as you deserve, I will not sweep you clean away" (46:28, NEB). Others will perish, but not you. After necessary correction you, my favored child, will prosper and flourish.

Chapter 16

THE TOLA TRIUMPH *

The Essence of Life: "Behold, the days are coming, says the Lord, when I will make a new covenant with the house of Israel and the house of Judah. . . . I will put my law within them, and I will write it upon their hearts; and I will be their God, and they shall be my people" (31:31-33).

"Mother, I shall always love the words of Jeremiah."

Miriam and her mother sit in their modest, yet comfortable, new home in a large Jewish settlement on the Chebar River near Babylon, after having left the hovel beside the Euphrates.

Having taken the advice of Jeremiah, many of the Hebrews settled down in this place and enjoyed a degree of prosperity as colonizers rather than captives. Daniel's growing influence at court, as well as Nebuchadnezzar's respect for Jeremiah, no doubt contributed to Jewish welfare.

Already Daniel, we assume, had looked into the fortunes of the Tola family and was able to render considerable help, especially when he learned that Tola had warmly supported the teachings of Jeremiah, whom Nebuchadnezzar held in high esteem. Now Rachel and Miriam are discussing the favorable turn events had taken.

After Miriam voices a love for Jeremiah, her mother replies, "Yes, my daughter, God is good to us. But I'm interested in knowing why you say it."

"He told us to seek the peace of this place, and in doing so we have found peace," replies the daughter.

Shimron, who has been scanning some valuable cloth he is selling, joins the conversation:

"I'm glad we always sought the advice of our parents. Think of where we might be if I had gone ahead with the plot to kill the Chaldean overlord."

---

*This chapter based on Jeremiah 48-51.

"I shudder to think of it," Miriam whispers.

Shimron adds, "And I'm thankful our parents were patient, wise, and kind, and that they followed the Sacred Words."

"They are gracious words," says Rachel. "There will be troubles, yes. But God always takes care of us."

Rachel then reads one of the prophet's declarations of peace that she has diligently gathered from the elders who communicate with Jeremiah in Jerusalem.

" 'In those days and in that time, says the Lord, the people of Israel and the people of Judah shall come together, weeping as they come; and they shall seek the Lord their God. They shall ask the way to Zion, with faces turned toward it, saying, "Come, let us join ourselves to the Lord in an everlasting covenant which will never be forgotten" ' " (50:4, 5).

Their conversation suddenly stops as they hear the sound of a horse. Bela, who works in the palace under Daniel's direction, springs from the saddle and rushes into the house.

"It's incredible! Absolutely marvelous!" Bela shouts as he comes in. "You won't believe it!"

"What's all this?" asks Miriam, startled and vastly intrigued. "Have you decided to get married?"

"No! No! Now sit down, and I'll tell you all about the biggest news that ever struck your gentle ears!"

To their wonderment he tells of an amazing event at the palace. Nebuchadnezzar had a strange dream that no one could explain. Finally, after seeking God for understanding, Daniel was able to make plain the whole mystery.

"The king fell on his face and paid homage to Daniel!" Bela exclaims. "And that wasn't all, by any means!"

Miriam, completely spellbound by the almost unbelievable story, urges, "Tell us. I can't wait to hear."

"He acknowledged our God as supreme," the excited youth continues. "This is what he said to Daniel: 'Truly, your God is God of gods and Lord of kings, and a revealer of mysteries' " [Daniel 2:47].

"Happy day! Oh, happy day!" interjects Rachel. "Didn't our prophet tell us this would happen some day? Listen to his words:

" 'I will make them honored, and they shall not be small'

[30:19]. 'Again I will build you, and you shall be built, O virgin Israel!' [31:4]. 'They shall be radiant over the goodness of the Lord' " [31:12].

"But there's still more," Bela announces, "much more!" He pauses to bait their curiosity, already at the breaking point.

"Daniel has been appointed ruler of the entire province of Babylon and chief prefect over all the wise men of Babylon," says Bela in a cool, steady voice that only accentuates the overwhelming impact of the disclosure.

So in this construction of fancy—based, nonetheless, on the facts of the case—let us now finish the happy story of the triumph of the House of Tola.

Daniel investigates the events surrounding his kinsmen. The cruel overlord is demoted and in disgrace sent to a minor post at a grim frontier station where, after months of brooding, he takes his own life.

Daniel conducts all the Tolas on a tour of the palace, and they marvel at the sights of a magnificent structure with hanging gardens. Bela is made chief assistant to Daniel. Shimron is entrusted with an important post in the imperial government. Miriam, who long before broke with Asher, marries a devoted Hebrew in Daniel's office. Rachel enjoys years of honor, spending many happy days with her grandchildren. She is regarded by the exiles as a sort of high priestess of the ancient faith and a custodian of Jeremiah's letters.

Back in Jerusalem, in real life, the prophet lifts his voice against nation after nation which has passed the limits of God's forbearance. The Book of Jeremiah is not written in connected order. Each chapter deals with revelations or events in the past that Baruch recorded or the prophet dictated to him, sometimes years after the occasion. So from the announcement of Nebuchadnezzar's coming conquest of Egypt in chapter 46, the record goes on through chapter 51, citing national ruin extending from Palestine to Babylon itself.

Moab is to be broken. Ammon will become a desolate heap; Edom a desolation like Sodom and Gomorrah. Damascus will wax feeble, no longer the proud city of praise and joy. Kedar ruined,

Hazor a desolation forever, and Elam stricken. But to Babylon is reserved the greatest wrath of all. Two entire chapters (50, 51), with 110 verses, tell of her judgments to come.

Her glory vanishes, her wealth and power fade, as oblivion falls upon the great center of tyranny and heathen mysticism. Forever after it becomes a symbol of that which is false in religion. The Book of Revelation, written by John, for instance, uses the figure extensively.

After accomplishing its destined work of chastising Israel and other nations, she must in turn be brought to account.

> "Babylon was a golden cup in the
>   Lord's hand,
>   making all the earth drunken;
>   the nations drank of her wine,
>   therefore the nations went mad" (51:7).

All nations were forced to drink from Babylon's cup of fury, but now she must in turn be broken. The prophet foresees her end: "Suddenly Babylon has fallen and been broken; wail for her!" (51:8). So complete is to be her destruction that no man will abide there (50:40). Today the great, proud city is a complete ruin, a place for archaeological diggings and a source of bricks for the surrounding area.

The cardinal sins of all these heathen nations were tyranny, drunkenness, immorality, and false religion. It was chiefly perverted religion in the case of Israel.

Daniel and his friends demonstrated the high priority God puts on control of appetite, a problem men have always faced. The gormandizing syndrome today attests to the fact. Taste control, or lack of it, is the chief factor in drinking and in overeating. When millions starve, it is a matter of self-serving to squander the bounties of nature upon oneself.

Time magazine (June 26, 1972, p. 51) gives some startling figures about the problem: "The quest for permanent slimness is rarely rewarding." It is pointed out that some doctors treating obese patients find that only twelve out of a hundred lose significant amounts of weight after being treated a year. And then comes this amazing conclusion: Out of the twelve, ten usually regain their weight during the following year, leaving only two out of one hundred as successfully treated. This observation is made: "It is easier to dry out drunks than to starve down heavy eaters."

Actually a cream pie and a cup of wine in some cases are almost equally guilty in the confrontation of taste control. Both are often involved in emotional problems. Motivation is the answer. Lack of motivation led the ancients to cross the forbidden frontier in Jeremiah's day. Time never seems to eliminate the challenge.

Like the Hebrews in Babylon, those who bring their lives into harmony with God's plan of living reap rich benefits. Said the prophet:

"The Lord has brought forth our vindication;
       come, let us declare in Zion
       the work of the Lord our God" (51:10).

"But it never seems to happen in my life," we are prone to say. Days, sometimes years, bring no change in an unsatisfactory situation.

This is the very point to observe in Israel's captivity. Things did not change overnight. Faith, trust, patience, were required of those who believed God. Serving Him is not a matter of snapping the finger and seeing magic wonders appear at once. Even nature testifies to this divine formula. Seed is planted; many weeks pass before the harvest. Birth comes after a mother has carried an infant for months. Trust. Believe. Wait. God's Word never fails.

Chapter 17

SET UPON MY LIPS A SONG*

The Essence of Life:

"Let my tongue cling to the roof of my mouth

if I do not remember you,

if I do not set Jerusalem

above my highest joy" (Psalm 137:6, NEB).

" 'Sing us one of the songs of Zion' " (Psalm 137:3), demanded the captors, no doubt charmed by the sublime beauty of the psalms.

Amid the barbaric splendors of Babylon the superiority of the Jewish heritage seemed apparent to the discerning. With demoniac dexterity the priests and magicians of Babylon had learned all the tricks of the trade. The whole system, guided by caprice or delusion, could not hold a candle to the simple beauty of the pure Hebrew faith.

It is little wonder, then, that we have the pathetic cry of Psalm 137:4 (NEB): "How could we sing the Lord's song in a foreign land?"

"Be merry. Give us music; we like to hear it," urged the citizens of the proud city that is now rubble and utter silence.

"How can we explain it to you?" replied the pathetic captives. "The cause of our sorrow takes away our song."

"By the rivers of Babylon we sat down and wept

when we remembered Zion.

There on the willow-trees

we hung up our harps" (Psalm 137:1, 2, NEB).

But in their distress they learned the sweet lessons of adversity. Clear and true came the warnings, the admonitions, and the comforts of Jeremiah, which greatly softened the effect of a rigorous exile.

---

*This chapter based on Jeremiah 27; 28; 21.

89

In Palestine the prophet continued to warn everyone against any attempts to resist Babylon at this time. Ambassadors from the surrounding nations, Zedekiah—the puppet king Nebuchadnezzar had appointed—all were given the words Jeremiah prophesied in Jerusalem.

He was commanded to put a yoke on his neck. This represented the king of Babylon, whom the people of Judah must serve until his own destined time came. Resistance would be futile. Contrasted to their internal weakness, Babylon possessed too much strength. "Do not listen," he urged, "to your prophets, your diviners, your wise women, your soothsayers, and your sorcerers when they tell you not to serve the king of Babylon" (27:9, NEB).

These astral projections, esoteric mysticisms, occult incantations, witchcraft perceptions, psychic tours into subterranean caverns of devilism, will only bring trouble.

All the modern occult phenomena contain the same elements Jeremiah challenged. It was part of the cultism that led to the demise of Babylon, so vividly portrayed by the prophet. Says *Time:* "The astrology so many millions follow today is a direct legacy from the astronomer priests of Babylonia" (June 19, 1972, p. 65).

Jeremiah's presence intervened between wrong tendencies and a crisis that would spell tragic ruin. He seemed to say: "Preserve your pure heritage—the faith of the fathers. Don't get involved in the lies of false prognosticators. Stay alert to the danger. Shun the temptation to follow attractive panaceas that offer nothing. It's all for your own good."

Amid the oppressive atmosphere of hostility, skepticism, and criticism, he set himself no less a task than to keep a segment of the world intact.

"Why should you and your people die?" (27:13, NEB), he asked Zedekiah. Do not listen to the false prophets, who advocate an uprising against Nebuchadnezzar. They tell lies. They are giving a false sense of security, and it will lead straight to disaster. Don't let them push you into a crisis or lull you into the sleep of death.

But there were other voices in Jeremiah's time, just as there are today. One bold voice contradicting the prophet from Anathoth was that of a certain Gibeonite named Hananiah, the son of Azzur.

At a large gathering he announced, "These are the words of the Lord of Hosts the God of Israel: I have broken the yoke of the king of Babylon. Within two years I will bring back . . . all the exiles" (28:2-4, NEB).

"May it be so!" Jeremiah replied cynically.

Dubiously he suspected a conspiracy. Here was one of the professional prophets, a man of striking personality, apparently sincere, riding a wave of popularity. Shocked, Jeremiah reminded those present that God had revealed the opposite to him. But here stood Mephistopheles himself. It would be like someone today suddenly encountering a spiritualist medium after studying the Biblical position on the dead.

He withdrew, somewhat perplexed, but God soon revealed to him the hoax. He received another kind of message for Hananiah ben Azzur of Gibeon:

"Listen, Hananiah. The Lord has not sent you, and you have led this nation to trust in false prophecies. Therefore these are the words of the Lord: Beware, I will remove you from the face of the earth; you shall die within the year" (28:15, 16, NEB).

Two months later Hananiah died.

Says W. H. Bennett in the *Expositor's Bible:* "Jeremiah was anxious that Zedekiah should keep faith with Nebuchadnezzar, and not involve Judah in useless misery by another hopeless revolt. The prophets preached the popular doctrine of an imminent Divine intervention to deliver Judah from her oppressors. They devoted themselves to the easy task of fanning patriotic enthusiasm, till the Jews were ready for any enterprise, however reckless" (*The Book of Jeremiah: Chapters XXI-LII*, p. 115).

For eight years Zedekiah kept his vow of loyalty to Babylon. Once he made a journey there to reaffirm his fidelity (51:59). But the conspiracy of the Syrians and Palestinians appealed to him after Egypt pledged strong support. Ignoring the vehement warnings of Jeremiah, the nation plunged headlong into the rebellion.

The Chaldeans assembled a powerful army and took to the field. The die had been cast; Jerusalem prepared for the expected siege. As the mighty forces of Babylon took up their positions

Zedekiah sent a delegation to Jeremiah, hoping for the miracle his counselors promised would happen.

"Nebuchadnezzar king of Babylon is making war on us," stated the officers; "inquire of the Lord on our behalf. Perhaps the Lord will perform a miracle as he has done in past times" (21:2, NEB).

It amounted to undiluted presumption. We read in 2 Chronicles 36 the real condition of king and people.

"He did what was evil in the sight of the Lord his God. He did not humble himself before Jeremiah the prophet, who spoke from the mouth of the Lord. . . . All the leading priests and the people likewise were exceedingly unfaithful, following all the abominations of the nations; and they polluted the house of the Lord which he had hallowed in Jerusalem. . . . But they kept mocking the messengers of God, despising his words, and scoffing at his prophets, till the wrath of the Lord rose against his people, till there was no remedy" (2 Chronicles 36:12-16).

A crestfallen, bitter delegation, haunted by fear, went back to the king. Jeremiah told them in no uncertain terms just what to expect. Nebuchadnezzar would surely triumph. But there remained a glimmer of hope.

"You shall say further to this people, These are the words of the Lord: I offer you now a choice between the way of life and the way of death. Whoever remains in this city shall die by sword, by famine, or by pestilence, but whoever goes out to surrender to the Chaldaeans, who are now besieging you, shall survive; he shall take home his life, and nothing more" (21:8, 9, NEB).

The moment of decision had come. Jerusalem faced her last chance. It was now or never.

Said Longfellow in *Masque of Pandora* (part III):

"Decide not rashly. The decision made
Can never be recalled. The Gods implore not,
Plead not, solicit not; they only offer
Choice and occasion, which once being passed
Return no more. Dost thou accept the gift?"

God is always providing a way out—a fine rare essence of His goodness. Because of this the faithful can sing the sweet old songs of hope and joy, though the roads are blocked and bridges down.

Chapter 18

A CITY CALLED JOY*

The Essence of Life: "Behold, I will bring to it health and healing, and I will heal them and reveal to them abundance of prosperity and security" (33:6).

"Alas, lord!"

People would thus bewail the fate of King Zedekiah, according to what Jeremiah told him. Jerusalem would be taken and put to the torch. This, however, was only half the story. The other half involved a gleaming, smiling, happy place: the city called Joy.

Now comes one of Jeremiah's most noble acts—cited in chapter 34. He persuaded the king to liberate all the Hebrew slaves. The Chaldean menace induced Zedekiah to make the proclamation as a means of earning God's favor and the prophet's approval.

What rejoicing was heard in the city as the poor slaves and bond servants suddenly found themselves free! But it amounted to an empty gesture, a cynical act, as events soon proved. Like people who pray when danger threatens but turn back to their old ways after it blows over, the slaveholders rescinded the proclamation of liberty as an Egyptian army approached and the siege temporarily lifted.

Jeremiah's response was immediate and emphatic as the weak king did nothing. "Hypocrites!" cried the prophet. In the name of God he announced, " 'Behold, I proclaim to you liberty to the sword, to pestilence, and to famine' " (34:17).

He went on to tell them that the Chaldeans would turn back the Egyptians, then return and take the city. God's judgments against their perfidy and treachery could not be delayed much longer. What Jeremiah told the doomed city is something all men must ponder: God scrutinizes every act, whether good or bad, and his evil deeds will sooner or later catch up with a man.

A letter to Ann Landers tells how a husband phoned from another city, giving his wife the excuse that he had missed the

---

*This chapter based on Jeremiah 34; 32; 33.

plane. A chain of remarkable coincidences followed. That night his wife, relatives, and friends in various neighboring cities watched a hockey match on television. A wild puck flew into the stands, injuring a spectator. The camera focused on the victim. Sitting right next to the injured person and clearly cast on the television screen sat the guilty husband with his arm around a woman. The court later gave him a hard time.

Jerusalem demonstrated how God casts men and nations on a screen of infinite omniscience. No one escaped. The scrutiny could not be avoided. Jeremiah continually tried to get his countrymen to accept the fact, but they resisted his appeals. The leaders put him in jail for prophesying a Chaldean return and eventual victory.

In chapter 32 the prophet is instructed to lift a palm branch of hope and promise over his beleaguered people. It is revealed to him that a cousin will come with an offer to sell his field in Anathoth.

And who should appear in the court of the prison but this cousin, named Hanamel.

"Buy my field," said he.

"I'll do it."

The prophet thus confirmed the confidence he had in the future. In other words, he bought stock when the market had plunged to its lowest level. Though the nation was going down, he envisioned a future day of prosperity: "Houses and fields and vineyards shall again be bought in this land" (32:15).

The divine purpose is clear: Endure your troubles, and a grand new day awaits you. Don't doubt it, for God Himself says so. "I will rejoice in doing them good |think of it—God taking special pleasure in heaping good things upon us!|, and I will plant them in this land in faithfulness, with all my heart and all my soul |He puts all His boundless power and goodness into the sublime project!|. . . . So I will bring upon them all the good that I promise them" (32:41, 42).

A lantern glows in the darkness. God has a plan; be patient. But the people of Jerusalem did not want to wait for the divine purpose to mature, so they impatiently took matters into their own hands and ran straight into a hornet's nest of trouble. It was like a typical person today, or any day, confronted by stresses and frustrations, who becomes a psychosomatic case.

Confined to her home, without outside interests, a wife vents hostility on her husband and children—although she loves them dearly.

She hates pots and pans, wishes the diaper days would end sooner. Not being the dependent type who can adjust to staying happily at home, she finally begins to complain of headaches and back pains as an emotional reaction or outlet.

"It hurts," she groans.

"Yes, we know it hurts," her husband and friends comfort, but they find themselves unable to do much about the problem.

Many people caught in such a trap have found a way out by applying the method Jeremiah used in chapter 33 to alleviate the many aches and pains of Judah.

First came communication. "The word of the Lord came to Jeremiah . . . while he was still shut up |in prison|" (33:1). Husbands and wives can patiently talk their way out of emotion-producing situations, then apply the things that relieve stress and frustration. Participation in some church-sponsored activity has met the need for many families.

Then comes the greatest calmer and healer of all: prayer. Said God to Jeremiah as he spent time in prison for the faith he would not yield under any amount of pressure: " 'Call to me and I will answer you, and will tell you great and hidden things which you have not known' " (33:3). So it means great days ahead, even though you rot in jail today.

But hope rises. The Depression Healer takes over. Break down the city today, but it will rise again tomorrow. The backaches of frustration, the headaches of a diseased imagination, will be solved.

"Behold, I will bring to it health and healing, and I will heal them and reveal to them abundance of prosperity and security" (33:6).

In verse 9 we find the glory, the soft healing influence of hope in a better future—made all the more satisfying because God says it.

"And this city shall be to me a name of joy, a praise and a glory before all the nations of the earth" (33:9).

Jerusalem, as the prophet looked ahead, was slated to be a city called Joy. To a degree it became that in the Restoration. But God has many cities of joy. The grandest of all, of course, is the New Jerusalem, where happiness never fades. Every home also can become a little city called Joy. But it takes careful planning and much well-directed effort. No one ever heard of a city built without work and much thought.

Continuing the analogy of the home as a city called Joy, note chapter 33, verses 10 and 11:

"There shall be heard again the voice of mirth and the voice of gladness, the voice of the bridegroom and the voice of the bride, the voices of those who sing, as they bring thank offerings to the house of the Lord:

'Give thanks to the Lord of hosts,

for the Lord is good,

for his steadfast love endures for ever!' "

"The voice of gladness" will make the home a little piece of the New Jerusalem transferred to this earth. But it takes dedication and effort.

"The voices of those who sing"—junk the jerky blaring rock, and fill the home with soothing melody. It's worth investing money in the music that calms the soul and makes one serenely happy.

Jeremiah's next formula for healing and tranquillity introduces the Great Physician, the Comforter, the Pacifier.

"And this is the name by which it will be called: 'The Lord is our righteousness' " (33:16).

The city of joyful restoration came after seventy years of captivity. The New Jerusalem, city of joy complete, is the far-off but certain hope of all who believe. The home—also a city called Joy—is instant joy; men can have it now if they will. It is guaranteed to heal half the ills afflicting mankind.

Jeremiah always spread hope and a bright future into the littered, broken streets of the sordid city he denounced. All the little cities called Joy pave their shining boulevards with the same golden stones of joyful anticipation.

The pleasant promises are irrevocable. God has given His

word. Every man can depend upon it. Life exudes a sweet essence of the best joys when the Word is loved, honored, and followed. The glowing chapter of Jeremiah 33 closes with a declaration that the return of day and night will fail before God breaks His covenant of peace and security. That makes it just about as certain as anything Jeremiah or anyone else ever thought about in this changing world.

And the most difficult situations often prove the most rewarding. Samuel Smiles wrote: "A distinguished investigator in physical science has left it on record that, whenever in the course of his researches he encountered an apparently insuperable obstacle, he generally found himself on the brink of some discovery. The very greatest things—great thoughts, discoveries, inventions—have usually been nurtured in hardship, often pondered over in sorrow, and at length established with difficulty" (*Self-help*, p. 322).

Chapter 19

THE TWILIGHT OF JUDAH*

The Essence of Life:
>   "You shall hear a cry of terror. . . .
>   Awful is that day:
>   when has there been its like?
>   A time of anguish for Jacob,
>   yet he shall come through
>   it safely" (30:5, 7, NEB).

Good people always have their trouble being good. How are they to avoid the pitfalls? They should insulate themselves against the influence and companionship of bad people who despise and ridicule the good.

This was the trouble with Zedekiah, Judah's last tragic king. Like seeing a gleam of light in the gathering darkness, he heard the voice of Jeremiah pointing out the one way that would have saved him and his crumbling kingdom. But he had no mind of his own. The pro-Egyptian palace clique—the men who hated Jeremiah—took control of him. Vanity, stupidity, and delusion took the place of discretion and common sense.

>   "Earth, turning from the sun, brings night to man;
>   Man, turning from his God, brings endless night."
>   —Young, *Night Thoughts*

Then came the twilight of the Jews, the vast fearful chaos of extinction. The light went out, and darkness fell upon the land.

Jeremiah contrived to go along a dangerous path. It amounted to a choice between mounting antagonism and a life of silent discretion or escapism. He held the only key to national survival. But the men in charge would not listen to him. Nonetheless, he set himself to go along the difficult path of impossible attainment. Though failure appeared inevitable, he continued to oppose the war party. "You're headed for the abyss!" he cried.

---

*This chapter based on Jeremiah 37-39; 52:1-30.

But the false prophets and the confused leaders gloated that the Egyptians would take care of them. "God is on our side. Victory is ours!"

"Not so," declared Jeremiah. "Pharaoh's army which marched out to help you is on its way back to Egypt, its own land, and the Chaldaeans will return to the attack. They will capture this city and burn it to the ground. These are the words of the Lord: Do not deceive yourselves, do not imagine that the Chaldaeans will go away and leave you alone. They will not go; for even if you defeated the whole Chaldaean force with which you are now fighting, and only the wounded were left lying in their tents, they would rise and burn down the city" (37:7-10, NEB).

To their dismay, the defenders of Jerusalem soon found out that the prophet was right. The Chaldeans returned and began the swift, terrible work of totally crushing the revolt.

In some ways it was like the "empty nest syndrome" some psychologists today term the middle-years problems of life. Children have been raised, disenchantment sets in as some expectations have not been realized, and dread of old age begins, accompanied by feelings of insecurity. Husband and wife get tired of each other.

"You're not the same man I married," says one.

"You're not the pretty, loving girl I married," comes the reply.

Modern permissiveness and lack of respect for Biblical prohibitions lure one or both to try extramarital ventures. These experimentations backfire, and since divorce is no longer frowned upon as in former times, lawyers are brought into the scene. Thus a city of hope and a refuge sealed with a vow of faithfulness becomes another wreck on the disintegrating landscape of society.

The same solution would have solved both situations: the modern home and ancient Jerusalem. Sincere, honest efforts to order the life after the divine pattern, which means repentance and heart-searching, is the most potent formula for those spiritual conditions that can be traced to the human heart.

Jeremiah saw the hopelessness of trying to stop the mad rush toward the abyss; so he decided to leave the doomed city. Then Irijah, an officer of the guard, accosted him.

"You're a traitor; you're going over to the Chaldeans."

"It's a lie," Jeremiah answered.

But Irijah would not listen. Likely the prophet's arrest already had been agreed on; so Irijah brought him back, where the officers beat him and put him into a dungeon.

By now the Babylonians had increased their pressure, and Zedekiah displayed his characteristic indecision. He asked Jeremiah privately if there was a word from the Lord:

" 'Indeed there is,' " responded Jeremiah; " 'you shall fall into the hands of the king of Babylon. . . . Where are your prophets who prophesied that the king of Babylon would not attack?' " (37:17-19, NEB).

The princes now took a hand in dealing with this prophet who would not quiet his persistent warnings.

"The man must be put to death," they demanded. They contended he weakened the morale of the soldiers, probably a statement of truth in some cases. But the prophet really directed his words to the leaders whom he still hoped could be persuaded to see surrender as the only way out of the ultimate tragedy. They, however, clung to a fanatical belief that God would intervene to save the Temple, or perhaps Egypt would come to the rescue.

Zedekiah turned the prisoner over to their tender mercies; they lowered him into a death-pit, where he sank into the mud. Only when Ebed-melech, a Cushite, pleaded before Zedekiah, did the king save Jeremiah, who then was taken up and confined to the court of the prison.

Unwaveringly, Jeremiah held to the idea of surrender. He did not shirk the unpleasant, highly unpopular task of thus giving his people the one opportunity to save their lives.

Zedekiah's opportunity to live out a normal, prosperous life had been lost, but he still hoped for some crumbs of mercy that Jeremiah might possibly pick out of the sky for him. Therefore he arranged a secret meeting.

"I want to ask you something," said the troubled king; "hide nothing from me."

" 'If I speak out,' " replied Jeremiah, " 'you will certainly put me to death; if I offer you any advice, you will not take it' " (38:14, 15, NEB).

King Zedekiah vowed that Jeremiah would be safe.

"Jeremiah said to Zedekiah, 'These are the words of the Lord the God of Hosts, the God of Israel: If you go out and surrender to the officers of the king of Babylon, you shall live and this city shall not be burnt down; you and your family shall live. But if you do not surrender to the officers of the king of Babylon, the city shall fall into the hands of the Chaldaeans, and they shall burn it down, and you will not escape them' " (38:17, 18, NEB).

But the proud king hesitated. He feared men more than God.

The thought of their ridicule greatly bothered him as he pondered the prophet's offer.

" 'I am afraid of the Judaeans who have gone over to the enemy. I fear the Chaldaeans will give me up to them and I shall be roughly handled' " (38:19, NEB).

" 'They will not give you up,' " promised Jeremiah. " 'If you obey the Lord in everything I tell you, all will be well with you' " (38:20, NEB).

The way of obedience loomed hard and bitter to the king, who found it difficult to make up his mind, although he for the moment believed the prophet told him the exact truth. The lessons of obedience had not been learned well during the years, and now a strange hesitation immobilized his resolution.

General Robert E. Lee once sent an order to General Stonewall Jackson to come at his convenience to discuss matters that were not very urgent. Jackson rode at once through stormy weather to Lee's headquarters.

"I'm surprised to see you have come so soon," remarked Lee, "and especially in this weather. The matter wasn't urgent."

Jackson replied: "Your slightest wish is a supreme command for me. I always take pleasure in prompt obedience."

This kind of strict obedience, however, was something the Judean king did not practice. He procrastinated. But before dismissing the prophet he extracted a pledge to keep the interview secret. This Jeremiah observed, even though the officers tried to pry the information out of him.

King Zedekiah's indecision cost him and the nation dearly. After a siege of thirty months, in July 586 BC the Babylonians made a breach in the walls, through which the vengeful army of

Nebuchadnezzar rushed to sack the unhappy city. Even though Zedekiah managed to escape, he was captured, and what a fearful fate he suffered! His sons were slain before his eyes, then his eyes were put out before the Babylonians led him in chains to Babylon.

The nobles too who had been active in inciting the rebellion met their deaths at the hands of the vengeful Chaldeans. Thus ended forever the history of Jewish royalty in a vast carnage that Jeremiah strove to prevent. He wanted his countrymen to take another course, a new way which would have been shorn of pride and glory, perhaps, but nonetheless a safe one. The new Jeremiah we see in all of this is a man who steadfastly, at the cost of much suffering and scorn, strove to save a country that refused to be saved.

What of the fate of the prophet? "Nebuchadrezzar king of Babylon sent orders about Jeremiah to Nebuzaradan captain of the guard. 'Take him,' he said; 'take special care of him, and do him no harm of any kind, but do for him whatever he says.' So . . . all the chief officers of the king of Babylon . . . fetched Jeremiah from the court of the guard-house" (39:11-13, NEB).

He could have gone to Babylon and lived an honored life among the captives, a beneficiary of Nebuchadnezzar; but he chose to stay in Judea among the wretched remnants of a once proud nation.

They who save others are themselves saved. It is the very essence of the abundant life. Ebed-melech, the compassionate Cushite eunuch who saved the life of Jeremiah, received from the prophet a divine message of approbation: "I will keep you safe . . . because you trusted in me" (39:18, NEB).

No man ever really loses by trusting God.

Chapter 20

LIVE LONGER
AND LIVE BETTER *

The Essence of Life:
   "The steadfast love of the Lord
         never ceases,
      his mercies never come to an end;
   they are new every morning;
      great is thy faithfulness" (Lamentations 3:22, 23).

Following the peace settlement, events in Palestine moved from the ridiculous to the absurd. In place of the futile and unwise war conducted by Zedekiah, an uneasy peace of disorganized violence broke loose upon the land, after men had caught their breath.

Actually, the scattered remnant of Judah, by virtue of a new environment, should have entered an era of individual longevity and prosperity. Jerusalem, with its sordid city streets, lay in ruins, so the people were scattered abroad among country surroundings. Life became less complicated in many ways. The war with its excitement and tension, which had gone on for years, appeared over, and the Chaldeans were cast more in the role of protector than enemy.

The curtain had fallen on the old Jewish nation, and new actors appeared to play their part upon the vacant stage. Gedaliah, a friend of Jeremiah, was appointed governor, and a new era for the province seemed imminent as the scattered people flocked to his headquarters at Mizpah.

To all, including Jeremiah, resorting thither, a bright day appeared about to dawn. For a while all went well. Dared they hope this would mark the beginning of the joyful restoration revealed many times before to Jeremiah? Stress, worry, and insecurity

---

*This chapter based on Jeremiah 40-43:1-7.

diminished. Life indeed seemed to be getting better for the battered people.

An essay published in *Time* (July 10, 1972, pp. 64, 65) shows how people everywhere can live better and longer. After acknowledging the role of overeating, cholesterol, nicotine, and alcohol in shortening life expectancy among Americans, the findings pointed to worry, overwork, and stress as seriously affecting how long people live. Studies have found, for instance, that Jews in Israel have a lesser rate of heart disease than their brothers in the U.S. The same applies to the Japanese in the U.S. and Japanese in Japan.

Jeremiah and the remnant of Judah left in their homeland could reasonably expect a less involved and less stressful life, centering in Mizpah. But like this world in every age, just when things began to look better, the ugly ghost of trouble again made its horrendous appearance.

Johanan, one of the Jewish military leaders, discovered that Ishmael, a former noble at Zedekiah's court and probably a persecutor of Jeremiah, had put together a diabolical plot to kill Gedaliah.

"He is plotting to take your life," said Johanan to the governor, who was beginning—with Jeremiah's encouragement—to get a new order of things under way.

The trusting governor, however, did not believe the report. Absurd! This is just plain malice and jealousy. "You are speaking falsely of Ishmael," he said (see 40:16).

This credibility gap proved fatal to Gedaliah and the future course of the budding colony. Ishmael and his zealots murdered the governor, many of his adherents, and a number of Babylonian soldiers.

Like cool and hot air meeting in the sky, the elements of storm again broke upon the unhappy land. Johanan struck back furiously, eliminating the rebels but in turn introducing a dangerous new policy that started a debate as vehement as any preceding it.

Johanan reasoned that the Babylonians, not noted for patience or mercy, would hold all the nation guilty and without discrimination punish those responsible for the rebellion.

"Flee to Egypt!" became the cry as everyone, from the least to the greatest, was seized by panic. Coming to Jeremiah, they asked him to intercede for divine guidance. "We will obey the voice of the Lord," they vowed. For ten days they waited while the prophet supplicated the Lord. Then the message came, but it did not conform to the mingled hopes and fears that drew his hearers toward the fertile land, the riches, and the apparent security of Egypt.

" 'If you will remain in this land, then I will build you up and not pull you down; I will plant you, and not pluck you up. Do not fear the king of Babylon, of whom you are afraid; do not fear him, says the Lord, for I am with you, to save you and to deliver you from his hand. I will grant you mercy, that he may have mercy on you and let you remain in your own land' " (42:10-12).

In other words, don't run away from your problem. Jehovah has a new and gracious purpose awaiting you. He has a good plan, but you fret because it doesn't suit your purpose. What you really want is for Him to bend toward your own thinking, like the little girl in a buggy who tried to catch a wasp.

"No! No!" the nurse insisted.

The girl began to cry.

"Oh, let her have it," called the indulgent mother, annoyed, impatient, and too occupied with herself to investigate the cause.

Then came a shattering scream.

"What's the matter now?" groaned the mother.

"She caught the wasp—she got what she wanted."

Jeremiah in Lamentations stated the attitude of heart and soul that would have assured prosperity and security for the people who were always reaching for the bright-winged attractions in Egypt.

"It is good that one should wait quietly
for the salvation
of the Lord" (Lamentations 3:26).

After giving them God's promise, Jeremiah next repeated the old warning:

"But if you say, 'We will not remain in this land, . . . no, we will go to the land of Egypt, where we shall not see war . . . or be hungry, . . . then hear the word of the Lord, O remnant of Judah,' " (42:13-15).

In no uncertain terms the prophet informed them that this act of disobedience would only bring upon them the very things they feared. But the ghost of the past hung in the air like a dark presence. All the "insolent men," including Johanan, accused Jeremiah:

"You are telling a lie. The Lord our God did not send you to say, 'do not go to Egypt to live there'; but Baruch the son of Neriah has set you against us, to deliver us into the hand of the Chaldeans, that they may kill us or take us into exile in Babylon" (43:2, 3).

On the all-important point of remaining in Judah, which Jeremiah held to, the unbelieving remnant seemed unable to give any ground at all. Thus they forfeited the promise and headed straight for the forbidden land of the elusive hope and the fascinating illusion. Once more Jeremiah's fortunes changed, as had happened before when Josiah passed from the scene. Yesterday he was the confidant and guide of a new governor who could have brought prosperity to Judah—today he found himself in the hands of men who despised him. But again he refused compromise of a kind he considered irresponsible or self-serving.

How did things come to this pass? Jeremiah could have been instructed to warn Gedaliah of the conspiracy and thus opened his eyes to the danger. Instead, the prophet remained silent, and a bright hope of Judah perished in sulfurous fury.

It demonstrates the inscrutable wisdom, the often mysterious ways, of the infinite God. The divine purpose involved Babylon alone as the cleansing agent, a shield, and the prelude to future glory. When rebellious elements in Judah resisted this purpose, they courted disaster.

Unlike astrologers who shrewdly guess about everything from politics to earthquakes and often miss, Jeremiah remained silent on political matters and pronounced the one thing all Israel must do to enjoy divine favor. Knowing the intolerance and obstinacy of his people, he nonetheless bore his messages with undiminished constancy, regardless of the violent reaction.

"And they came into the land of Egypt, for they did not obey the voice of the Lord. And they arrived at Tahpanhes" (43:7).

The confused people, having refused the only sensible course, really did not know what they wanted. One may compare it to this incident:

A little girl asked her father for a nickel. When he offered her a five-dollar bill, she refused because she did not know its value.

"I don't want it. I want a nickel," she insisted.

Said the prophet in Lamentations 2:13:

> "What can I say for you, to what
> compare you,
> O daughter of Jerusalem?
> What can I liken to you, that I
> may comfort you,
> O virgin daughter of Zion?"

Though His child has rebelled, Jehovah desires to comfort the straying daughter. In the next verse the word *restore* is used.

Once Jerusalem, the virgin daughter, stood pure and unblemished, but now men say:

> " 'Is this the city which was called
> the perfection of beauty,
> the joy of all the earth?' "
> (Lamentations 2:15).

Yet the ideal, the glowing hope of the future, still stands if the daughter returns, repentant and purified, thus restored to the Father of love and compassion.

Moreover, it is pleasant to think of the virgin daughter taking the hand of someone else and saying, "Come, let us go and live with the loving Father."

Thus the divine purpose is realized. The joy and assurance of celestial wonders burst upon the mind, and everyone who chooses becomes a member of the royal family of God.

The undiminished glory of the Eternal will enlighten the redeemed as Christ, the Crucified One, leads them into the joys of God's everlasting Paradise. Jeremiah strove to save his deluded people. Christ calls all to come to Him and enjoy eternal life where wonders never cease.

Chapter 21

THE FURY AND THE GLORY*

The Essence of Life:
> "Let us test and examine our ways,
>   and return to the Lord!
>   Let us lift up our hearts and hands
>   to God in heaven" (Lamentations 3:40, 41).

Comes now the "reverse exodus" into Egypt. A disgrace indeed of men without faith. Re-creating what one of the refugees might have said, we hear this:

"Welcome, O Egypt, sweet land of plenty! Let us live and be glad while we are here."

But Jeremiah was there too. "God is against you!" he cried.

Nothing—and there must have been some who tried to weaken his dedication by flattery, if not by scorn—could conciliate his implacable resolve or temper his indomitable spirit. Commanded to set large stones in cement at Tahpanhes, he stated that the king of Babylon would come and spread his power over them. "He shall come and smite the land of Egypt" (43:11).

Defiantly bold, the displaced Jews resisted Jeremiah and blended idolatry with zeal for Jehovah. Their terrible experience had taught them nothing. "Then all the men who knew that their wives were burning sacrifices to other gods and the crowds of women standing by answered Jeremiah, 'We will not listen to what you tell us. . . . We will burn sacrifices to the queen of heaven' " (44:15-17, NEB).

This immoral worship, usually identified with the goddess Ishtar, roused the ire of Jeremiah. It corrupted the ancient Jews and persisted through the ages in one form or another: Ashtoreth, Diana, Venus. Venerated as the goddess of fertility, maternity, or sexual love, the rites often became grossly immoral. Sometimes her attributes were of a different nature, such as an intercessor for

---

*This chapter based on Jeremiah 43:8-13; 44; 52:31-34.

108

humanity before the gods, a characteristic that made the doctrine of the virgin Mary popular among half-heathen masses in Roman times.

Jeremiah gave up his people in Egypt as just about hopeless.

"How dulled is the gold,

how tarnished the fine gold!" (Lamentations 4:1, NEB).

We hear nothing of herosim in Egypt, except for the persistent courage and honesty of Jeremiah. Future glory lay with the captives at Babylon and their descendants—Daniel, Esther, Ezra, Nehemiah. Only in the East were God's purposes realized.

Jeremiah's glowing utterances were partially fulfilled in the case of Jehoiachin. The Book of Jeremiah closes with these words:

"In the thirty-seventh year of the exile of Jehoiachin king of Judah, on the twenty-fifth day of the twelfth month, Evil-merodach king of Babylon in the year of his accession showed favour to Jehoiachin king of Judah. He brought him out of prison, treated him kindly and gave him a seat at table above the kings with him in Babylon. So Jehoiachin discarded his prison clothes and lived as a pensioner of the king for the rest of his life. For his maintenance a regular daily allowance was given him by the king of Babylon as long as he lived, to the day of his death" (52:31-34, NEB).

But the glory of restoration, the enormous significance of Jeremiah's poetic and gracious forecasts, came to a people whose hearts were changed. Even the literal restoration under Ezra and Nehemiah pale before the brilliant burst of the New Covenant, pronounced by the prophet and fulfilled in Christ.

In Him rose the vision of splendor, the new revelation, the ultimate restoration. It came clear and sweet, like transparent waters flowing through the earth from the depths of celestial fountains. The sublime flash of glory lights up endless vistas, and every pain is healed.

The earliest missionaries to Japan used the Gospel of John to teach a young man who wanted to learn English. Soon he became deeply concerned and asked, "Who is this Man named Jesus? You call Him a man, but He must be God."

The Eternal Light is indeed the ultimate outreach of Jeremiah, the "iron pillar," who became the proclaimer of the tender mercies in the new covenant. Like a great river the Light flows gently among the green banks of the beautiful hope. Rising in the everlasting hills of righteousness, the sacred river bears the pledge of peace to the new Israel: "This is the covenant which I will make with the house of Israel after those days, says the Lord: I will put my law within them, and I will write it upon their hearts; and I will be their God, and they shall be my people" (31:33).

Thus Jeremiah is inseparably linked to Christ, the Messiah. The prophet's mission will reach full bloom when Christ returns: "They shall come with shouts of joy to Zion's height, shining with happiness at the bounty of the Lord." The exiles have returned, but complete restoration is still to come: "They shall become like a watered garden and they shall never want again" (31:12, NEB).

God loves His wayward children. "Is Ephraim still my dear son, a child in whom I delight?" Oh, yes. "I still remember him; and so my heart yearns for him, I am filled with tenderness towards him" (31:20, NEB).

Often in symbolic terms Jeremiah reveals the hidden riches of God's ways. Look at it this way: Symbolic terms add hidden value to the search. To discover a hidden mystery makes the object far more attractive. If gold were as common as iron, it would have little value.

My father and I once owned a gold mine in central Idaho. Our little gulch contained much of the yellow metal, but none could be seen by just walking over the ground. The hidden treasure had to be extracted by search and persistent digging. If gold could be gathered easily in buckets, it would not be worth much.

Only by deep study and earnest search do we find the hidden beauty of God's Word, hence the use of vivid symbolisms. Referring to the physical as well as spiritual beauty of God's people in their blameless state, the prophet used these similes:

"Her princes were purer than snow,
    whiter than milk;
  their bodies were more ruddy than coral,
    the beauty of their form was
      like sapphire" (Lamentations 4:7).

After his death, Jeremiah was recognized as one of Israel's greatest prophets. Many traditions sprang up about his later years and death. One had it that he was stoned to death in Egypt by the resentful Jews. Another transferred him to Babylon, where he spent his last days respected and honored by both Jews and Chaldeans. But most likely he lived out his days in Egypt and died a natural death.

Let us use our own imagination as we visualize the old prophet spending his declining and less active years at Tahpanhes in Egypt.

"The sands are number'd that make up my life;

Here must I stay, and here my life must end"

—Shakespeare, *III Henry VI*, Act I, scene IV

Few openly honor the old prophet. His countrymen usually dismiss him with a shrug, a joke, or a sneer. Yet they secretly admire his unquestioned courage and honesty. Any man who tells what he believes, even though others don't like to hear it, is always respected. But there are a few in Tahpanhes who regard the prophet with strong affection, and they greet him warmly as he passes with faltering steps toward a familiar spot on the eastern channel of the Nile as it flows through the lush delta.

We see him sitting there on the riverbank; he gazes serenely into the great stream, flowing, like human life to a silent sleep. Soliloquizing, he says, "The river knows its way to the sea. Without a human guide it moves along, blessing men with its ceaseless charity." Jeremiah also knows his way. Nothing—praise, flattery, or scorn—has turned him from his unshakable resolve to do God's will.

He sees the river flowing at his feet, and he touches its soothing water. But neither he nor anyone else in Egypt at that time knows where it comes from. That it starts from a great lake in central Africa is unknown to them. Yet he does not let the hidden mystery of its source bother him. Like his faith in the mysterious ways of Heaven, he accepts what he knows and leaves the rest to God. Misunderstood, persecuted, buffeted. So what? God knows all about it, and that is sufficient.

"Oh, river!" he could have cried, "you are never still. Your ancient flood never stops." Neither does Jeremiah cease his task to magnify God. Perseveringly, though crushed and battered, he keeps marching on.

Let us listen to the poetic feelings within him as we interpolate by borrowing from William Cullen Bryant's "The Night-Journey of a River":

> "Oh River, gentle River! gliding on
> In silence underneath this starless sky!
> Thine is a ministry that never rests
> Even while the living slumber."

It is not hard to picture Jeremiah beside the river, for it so much reflected his own life. His ministry never faltered. While he rushed upon men with the implacable yet loving fury of a spokesman for God, he did so in terms of a profound mission. They needed to be saved from themselves, and only he could shake them.

Finally, not far from where he sits, the Nile reaches the Mediterranean. Constant, the river flows into the changeless sea. Israel has changed, but not Jeremiah. He can be depended on to tell the truth regardless of weather or the stock market. God must be supremely pleased with such men.

Perhaps rushing through the prophet's mind are thoughts like those of Longfellow, in *Christus: A Mystery*, "The Golden Legend," part 1:

> "The Nile, forever new and old,
> Among the living and the dead,
> Its mighty mystic stream has rolled."

The aging prophet, contemplating the mighty stream, can understand the old and new. He called for men to live up to the old but ageless standards, and he extolled the beauty of the bright new day ahead as God reveals the matchless vistas of His covenant of everlasting peace. To us the new Jeremiah overshadows the old.

It matters not how long we live, but how. On this basis the ancient seer faced his last day among the living with calm and courage. By unfaltering trust he put one foot into the grave and then entered without fear.

The eternal call to rest rolls on. The old must go and new emerge. Between the worlds of birth and death man treads his path to shame or to glory. Let everyone look at this grand old man dying beside the Nile and resolve to emerge a new man of God emulating his heroic life!

Jeremiah was the supreme exponent of the scalpel and the bandage. He cut deep, but it was only to remove the tumor of evil. Then came the sweet essence of healing balm. He was God's master surgeon on the human soul.

The lines in Lamentations 3:31-33 give us the picture in right perspective of life as it really is:

> "For the Lord will not
> cast off for ever,
> but, though he cause grief, he will
> have compassion
> according to the abundance of
> his steadfast love;
> for he does not willingly afflict
> or grieve the sons of men."

So we can face our troubles as did Jeremiah and assert the same bold confidence: "Thou didst come near when I called on thee; thou didst say, 'Do not fear!' " (verse 57). This is in truth the sweet essence of life at its best, a bountiful life every man can know.

The iron prophet still stands, defiant and austere. Yet as the mist of hoary ages clears, there also emerges the image of a new Jeremiah, the man of a sensitive, tender heart, proclaiming to all men a new day of gentle love, of soft hope and bright promise. Repent and live. God is waiting to forgive. He hates sin and must deal with it, but He never ceases to love the sinner. No man ever portrayed this better than Jeremiah.

Chapter 22

THE DESERT SHALL BE GLAD

The Essence of Life:
>"O throne of glory, exalted from the beginning,
>   the place of our sanctuary,
>O Lord on whom Israel's hope is fixed"
>   (17:12, 13, NEB).

The captive Jews were carried from their land of milk and honey to the deserts of Babylonia. True, great rivers often caused the desert to bloom, yet the grim desolation of intense heat and lifeless earth encroached everywhere upon the gardens men had laboriously developed.

Thither came the exiles, not to suffer the dire vengeance of God's wrath but to receive corrective surgery. Jeremiah stated the case clearly. He did not concern himself so much with the philosophy and reason of their predicament but with its cause and effect. In plain, simple terms he said rebellion and apostasy would lead to serious trouble. Then he told them that the way to get out of their situation could be found by turning back to God.

The charge is explicit:
>"I will state my case against my people
>   for all the wrong they have done in forsaking me,
>   in burning sacrifices to other gods,
>   worshipping the work of their own hands" (1:16, NEB).

Why did God's people so persistently wander into these deplorable ways? Why such proclivity to dilute their pure and superior faith with the subtle corruptions of the heathen?

We can understand why by looking at ourselves today and find significant parallels.

The process of decline and departure begins with loss of the first love, or in other words, a fading of zeal, faith, and enthusiasm.

Said Jeremiah: "These are the words of the Lord:
I remember the unfailing devotion of your youth,

114

the love of your bridal days. . . .
Israel then was holy to the Lord,
    the firstfruits of his harvest" (2:2, 3, NEB).

The guidance of God and the unrivaled beauty of their faith should have inspired an unending zeal for Him. But they lost their enthusiasm and became indifferent to the pristine beauty of their religion. But God, whose love they shunned, pleaded through Jeremiah (2:4-7, NEB) for a return to the purity and devotion they once knew.

"Listen to the word of the Lord, people of Jacob, families of Israel, one and all. These are the words of the Lord:

What fault did your forefathers find in me,
    that they wandered far from me,
pursuing empty phantoms and themselves becoming empty;
that they did not ask, 'Where is the Lord,
    who brought us up from Egypt,
    and led us through the wilderness,
    through a country of deserts and shifting sands,
    a country barren and ill-omened, where no man ever trod,
    no man made his home?'
I brought you into a fruitful land
    to enjoy its fruit and the goodness of it;
    but when you entered upon it you defiled it
    and made the home I gave you loathsome."

Finally Israel lost the rich inheritance. By turning a deaf ear to God's pleas, voiced through the prophets, their zeal for truth declined as a fascination for heathen innovations increased.

"But my people have exchanged their Glory
    for a god altogether powerless.
    Stand aghast at this, you heavens,
    tremble in utter despair,
        says the Lord" (2:11, 12, NEB).

"Experience shows that success is due less to ability than to zeal," said Charles Buxton. "The winner is he who gives himself to his work, body and soul."

In many ways some among the Israel of God today are guilty of the same lack of zeal and wholehearted dedication to their peerless truth. The church of Laodicea in Revelation is generally conceded to symbolize the last believers on earth prior to the second coming of Jesus. "And unto the angel of the church of the Laodiceans write; . . . I know thy works, that thou art neither cold nor hot: I would thou wert cold or hot. So then because thou art lukewarm, . . . I will spue thee out of my mouth" (Revelation 3:14-16, KJV).

Lukewarmness induces a self-satisfied, indifferent, comfortable condition. When Jeremiah preached repentance, there was nothing but a big yawn, scorn, or business-as-usual attitude. Today general consent is given to the idea that Christ will come soon. But there is a noticeable lack of real enthusiasm, deep concern, or zealous preparation.

"Thou sayest, I am rich, and increased with goods, and have need of nothing" (verse 17, KJV). Never have Christian people been so blessed with material abundance as today. They are indeed "increased with goods." But there is a corresponding decrease in piety and zeal for the true riches of Christ. Because they possess so much, yet can show little spiritual plenty, they are destitute of the real values that endure: "Knowest not that thou art wretched, and miserable, and poor, and blind, and naked" (verse 17, KJV).

In Jeremiah's day the outward signs, displayed by a show of opulence, also betrayed inner poverty.

"And you, what are you doing?
　When you dress yourself in scarlet,
　　deck yourself out with golden ornaments,
　and make your eyes big with antimony,
　　you are beautifying yourself to no purpose" (4:30, NEB).

The voice of religion still rose in Jerusalem. Men cried, "Lord! Lord!" but it meant nothing when their acts betrayed a shallow profession. Jeremiah pointed this out: "Men may swear by the life of the Lord, but they only perjure themselves" (5:2, NEB).

In all of this there is an attitude of thinking more about pleasing men, acquiring possessions, pride, and display than of striving to win the blessing and favor of heaven. They told Jeremiah to keep quiet. "Go back to the olive groves, don't get worked up over what you think God told you, and stop irritating people."

An Indian heard a white man talk against others who showed that they took their religion seriously. "I don't know about all that," said the Indian, "but better for pot to boil over than pot not boil at all."

The Laodiceans are urged to acquire the riches of heaven that endure forever. "I counsel thee to buy of me gold tried in the fire, that thou mayest be rich; and white raiment, that thou mayest be clothed; . . . and anoint thine eyes with eyesalve, that thou mayest see" (Revelation 3:18, KJV).

One writer put it thus: "Whoever under the reproof of God will humble the soul with confession and repentance . . . may be sure that there is hope for him. Whoever will in faith accept God's promises, will find pardon. The Lord will never cast away one truly repentant soul" (E. G. White, *Patriarchs and Prophets*, p. 726).

Jeremiah voiced God's exhortation to Israel and Judah:

> "Learn your lesson, Jerusalem,
>   lest my love for you be torn from my heart,
>   and I leave you desolate" (6:8, NEB).

Today there comes to lukewarm Laodicea a sweet message of love amid all the trials and troubles of life—even for those who possess so much of the world's riches.

"As many as I love, I rebuke and chasten: be zealous therefore, and repent" (Revelation 3:19, KJV).

"Adversity has made many a man great who, had he remained prosperous, would only have been rich," said Maurice Switzer.

One can almost hear Jeremiah saying, "Come home, my wandering, starving brothers, to the Father's house. Sit down, feast at His bountiful table, and enjoy His boundless love."

This would be the real Jeremiah, voicing love in his heart for confused, unhappy people. In this he reflected how God feels about those who turn against Him. A spirit of greed had blinded the hearts of men, and this caused them to forget God and the needs of others. "From the least of them even unto the greatest of them every one is given to covetousness" (6:13, KJV). Get, get, and hold what you get.

"Mend your ways and your doings," admonished God through Jeremiah, "that I may let you live in this place. . . . Mend your ways, . . . deal fairly with one another, do not oppress the alien, the orphan, and the widow, . . . do not run after other gods to your own ruin" (7:3-6, NEB).

Thus the prophet showed the guilty nation how to avoid the terrible doom he predicted if it continued the headlong plunge into backsliding.

A similar appeal is graciously presented to the Laodiceans: the voice of Christ inviting them to turn from disgraceful backsliding to the only source of triumph and peace: "Behold, I stand at the door, and knock: if any man hear my voice, and open the door, I will come in to him, and will sup with him, and he with me" (Revelation 3:20, KJV).

"Do you have something for a cold?" inquired a man of the druggist.

"Did you bring a prescription?" asked the druggist.

"No, but I brought a bad cold."

When Jesus asks us to seek Him, all we need to bring is our own sinful selves. He will forgive and cure the evil in our lives. God stood ready to do just that when Jeremiah called Jerusalem to repentance.

A righteous indignation boiled in the prophet's soul when he saw the stubborn unbelief and determined rebellion of Israel: "I am full of the anger of the Lord, I cannot hold it in" (6:11, NEB).

He scanned the spiritual landscape and did not like it. From high to low, everyone seemed bent on serving himself or lusting after the false gods of the land. The king, with the acquiescence of time-serving, weak-kneed priests, put himself at the head of a movement which cast doubt and skepticism on the primitive, untarnished truth of God. Fearlessly Jeremiah denounced that "prophets and priests are frauds, every one of them" (6:13, NEB).

What did he have against these leaders of the people who were failing in their task of healing the bruised souls of men, failing also to tell about the dire consequences of complacency in a time of imminent peril?

"They dress my people's wound, but skin-deep only,
with their saying, 'All is well' " (6:14, NEB).

Is that the way it is—will this suffice for the coming crisis?

"All well? Nothing is well!" (6:14, NEB).

How do these false shepherds react when told that they are like the blind leading the blind, without any sense of shame or responsibility?

"Are they ashamed when they practise their abominations? Ashamed? Not they!" (6:15, NEB).

Jeremiah tells them plainly what they can expect for all their persistent backsliding:

"Therefore they shall fall with a great crash,
  and be brought to the ground on the day of my reckoning.
    The Lord has said it" (6:15, NEB).

The prophet goes on to give the reason for the carelessness and indifference of the people: "They have given no thought to my words and have spurned my instruction" (6:19, NEB).

Yet to these rejecters of God's mercy a call to repentance is sounded. He warns them, implying that all will be well if they only listen to Him and mend their ways. "I will appoint watchmen to direct you; listen for their trumpet-call" (6:17, NEB).

The overcomers, those who gain power over the devil and the flesh, will also enjoy the rich blessings of heaven in the time of the Laodicean church: "To him that overcometh will I grant to sit with me in my throne, even as I also overcame, and am set down with my Father in his throne" (Revelation 3:21, KJV).

Jeremiah warned, "The foe, sword in hand, is a terror let loose" (6:25, NEB). Yet this flood of evil let loose upon the land of Judah and against the Laodiceans will be put down by the power of the Omnipotent. The terror itself will be used to enhance the strength of those who resist evil and obey God. Jeremiah gives the secret of success in the next chapter: "If you obey me, I will be your God and you shall be my people. You must conform to all my commands, if you would prosper" (7:23, NEB).

Instead of responding to Jeremiah's appeals in behalf of God, they took a self-serving course: "But they did not listen; they paid no heed, and persisted in disobedience with evil and stubborn hearts." "This is the nation that did not obey the Lord its God nor accept correction" (7:24, 28, NEB).

Those who accepted correction found gladness on the desert. God used adversity to produce beautiful gardens of the heart where once had been briers and thorns. From trial and struggle rose the overcomers who turned the desert into a delightful dwelling place. Babylon became the scene of glorious triumphs, where Daniel and his companions, along with many others, burnished by adversity, restored a bright luster to the ancient faith.

The overcomers today are going over some of the same ground as test and trial shake them out of the Laodicean sleep of death. A new look at Jeremiah reveals that all the hard things we endure are the necessary corrections God uses to make us strong for battle: the joyfully victorious overcomers, glad on the desert where once was nothing but bitter desolation and disappointment. The Lord's sole objective is to bring them to this happy destination. Confused, searching, hungry people are always kept in His sight. Reluctantly He must allow them to suffer so they will repent and then change their way of living.

It is a glimmer of this sublime purpose that appears in Alexander Solzhenitsyn's thinking as he writes his *Gulag Archipelago*.

Innocent of crime—except possibly political nonconformity—he languished in prison for seven years. In the seventh year, after self-examination, he seemed to reach the conclusion that deep within was a malignant moral tumor that taints everyone, and it must be eliminated by suffering. So he came out a better person, though he could not fully comprehend the mystery of it all. But the purpose was clear and understandable.

"I would not have murmured," he writes, "even if all that punishment had been considered inadequate" (*The Gulag Archipelago II*, p. 614).

An even higher purpose is found in God's way, for it prepares us for life eternal. Everything, even the bitter disappointments, is used by Him. Then with thanksgiving we shall walk among the blooming flowers where His grace has made the burning desert glad.

"All things work together for good to them that love God" (Romans 8:28, KJV).

Addressing Jeremiah, God said, "I have set thee for a tower and a fortress among my people" (6:27, KJV).

God and Jeremiah, looking at Jerusalem, exclaimed, "O daughter of my people!" (6:26).

To His people today He says, "He that hath an ear, let him hear" (Revelation 3:22, KJV).

Chapter 23

GOING HOME

The Essence of Life: "Jacob shall return, and shall be in rest, and be quiet, and none shall make him afraid" (30:10, KJV).

It is hard, heartbreakingly hard, to leave home as a captive exile. But how wonderfully joyful is the day of return—the thrilling moment of going home!

Jeremiah, of course, knew he would not be among the returnees, but he held out the hope as a bright promise to lift up flagging spirits during the seventy years of grinding captivity. One can endure almost anything when he knows the future will bring a change.

Throughout his whole life the courageous prophet remained loyal to the divine charge, thus becoming an example of how people should make God first in a materialistic world. A *New York Times* poll showed that most respondents thought materialism the greatest problem facing the United States. This materialistic emphasis also vexed the spirit of Jeremiah as he tried to reform his wayward countrymen. At times the task almost overwhelmed him.

"I am the man," he cried, putting in print how frustrated he felt about the utter obstinancy of people who refused to listen. "I am the man who has known affliction, I have felt the rod of his wrath" (Lamentations 3:1, NEB). From this cry we can see that he felt involved in the judgments falling upon his erring people, though they deserved none of his empathy.

"I have become a laughing-stock to all nations,
 the target of their mocking songs all day" (verse 14, NEB).

He longed for peace and acceptance, but none came to him as frustrating days stretched into years of scorn and rejection.

"Peace has gone out of my life,
 and I have forgotten what prosperity means.
 Then I cry out that my strength has gone
 and so has my hope in the Lord" (verses 17, 18, NEB).

Did Jeremiah really lose hope? Perhaps, when it came to expecting any chance, short of dire adversity, for Israel's reconciliation. But this versatile man recovered faith and courage because his confidence in God remained unshaken.

"All this I take to heart

and therefore I will wait patiently" (verse 21, NEB).

Though the future seems dark, providence overshadows all of man's tribulations. Patience will resurrect hope; but patience comes in the fires of affliction. Sandwiched between the groans of the buffeted seer come the lines of uplift, the unshadowed days of future deliverance.

"The Lord's true love is surely not spent

nor has his compassion failed;

they are new every morning,

so great is his constancy" (verses 22, 23, NEB).

Oh, yes, we had better believe it. God is the same; He changes not. The trouble is with us. Yet as Jeremiah prays, sometimes he wonders how effective his prayers really are. The long days stretch into longer nights waiting for the answers that never seem to come. At least in the low moments, when everything seemed to go against him, the faithful prophet waits for evidence of God's favor.

"Thou hast hidden thyself behind the clouds

beyond reach of our prayers."

"All our enemies . . . jeer at us" (verses 44, 46, NEB).

This is true concerning the rebellious nation. But like the clouds that pass and reveal a crystal sky, the suffering people, jeered by enemies, will once more gain the ear and blessings of God as pain leads to repentance. Time only confirmed the words of Jeremiah. The misery of his people touched the heart of the prophet. The innocent suffered with the guilty. The whole igneous situation moved the sensitive soul of Jeremiah, and he became the weeping prophet.

"My eyes run with streams of water

because of my people's wound" (verse 48, NEB).

Jeremiah suffered much because he bore God's message of fury to a guilty people. Tormented by the rage of the rulers, he endured days of lonely imprisonment or flight into the wilderness to save

his life. Sometimes his enemies seemed to triumph, and he waited
patiently for God to vindicate him.

>"Those who for no reason were my enemies
>drove me cruelly like a bird;
>they thrust me alive into the silent pit,
>>and they closed it over me with a stone;
>the waters rose high above my head,
>>and I said, 'My end has come.'
>But I called on thy name, O Lord,
>>from the depths of the pit;
>thou heardest my voice; do not turn a deaf ear
>>>when I cry, 'Come to my relief' "
>>>>(verses 52-56, NEB).

Though it often seemed he was abandoned to the plots, taunts,
injustice, and jeers of his enemies, God watched over His faithful
servant. The silent moments of despair kept him well honed and
disciplined for the glorious work he must do. As he kept the faith,
endured and compromised not a single inch, God's gentle voice
came with the sweetest assurance.

>"Thou wast near when I called to thee;
>>thou didst say, 'Have no fear.'
>Lord, thou didst plead my cause
>>and ransom my life" (verses 57, 58, NEB).

When John Paton was translating the Bible into one of the
South Sea languages, a word for *believe* always eluded him. He
listened carefully day after day but never heard the word he could
use. Then one day a native teacher, tired and hot, fell into a chair
in his study. He used a word which meant, "I'm resting all of my
weight here."

"That is the word!" exclaimed Paton. "Believing in Jesus is to
rest one's whole self on Him."

Although good men could still be found in Judah who quietly
supported Jeremiah, it seemed to him as if he stood alone. But that
very isolation increased his faith and dependence upon the divine.

The book Lamentations of Jeremiah is a plaintive expression of
the great prophet personalizing the tragedy of the nation and
voicing his own distress. The poem depicts sorrows of a ruined

nation and a captive people hoping for a day of relief after years of punishment for disloyalty. Jeremiah, confident that God's purpose will be accomplished, lifts this hope into a prayer for remembrance and for restoration in the final chapter of the book.

Yet the fifth and last chapter of Lamentations is a dirge of lament as the book ends in a negative and pathetic vein. Here too is an interesting variation of translation. In verse 21 the cry wells up from afflicted people: "Restore us to thyself, O Lord, that we may be restored! Renew our days as of old!"

The last words of Jeremiah (Lamentations 5:22) show how the subtle shades of language confront translators with problems.

The King James reads: "But thou hast utterly rejected us; thou art very wroth against us."

The Revised Standard leaves us dangling with a provocative question:

> "Or hast thou utterly rejected us?
>
> Art thou exceedingly angry with us?"

The New English Bible brings the entire drama to a close with a question of deduction, inference, or condition:

> "For if thou hast utterly rejected us,
>
> then great indeed has been thy anger against us."

Yet there is a unique agreement in the contrasts of the language problem that prevents any loss of precision. A declarative, a question, or a conditional are all wrapped up in one, suggesting moods that might have come over the prophet's mind, which in time would be made clear. One can read into each version a unique harmony of agreement and yet ponder the delicate variations of language. This could suggest the very nature of Jeremiah himself: a man of mystery, yet dramatically relevant and profoundly human. Perhaps Inspiration wanted us to ask all the questions, then say that God was in it no matter what.

If the end comes as an apparent negative, it is very close to the pattern of life for most people. We read the last line, and there is no visible sign of deliverance. So we have to wait patiently. Some probably called Jeremiah a total failure. And maybe, being human, he sometimes felt that way himself. His attempt to reform Jerusalem proved a failure. Most people despised him as a preacher, and he was run out of town on more than one occasion.

By public relations experts today he would be given a very low rating on influencing people.

But in the final assessment he stands among the greatest men who ever lived. God gave him a hard, unpopular mission, and he stood immovable as a granite rock in the face of storm and fury. Any person who lives right can find inspiration and comfort in Jeremiah when he feels time passed him by and his work seems a failure. The prophet confirms the fact that what God thinks of us is the real thing worth thinking about.

The glory of Jeremiah's work appeared after his death. The joy of the return to the homeland came in the first year of Cyrus, king of Persia, after the seventy years of captivity—"that the word of the Lord by the mouth of Jeremiah might be fulfilled" (Ezra 1:1, KJV).

The electrifying news spread through the abodes of the captives: "We are going home at last!" they exclaimed. The thousands who returned, however, did not find the old home a land overflowing with milk and honey. Ezra and Nehemiah were confronted by many difficulties and frustrations. Yet going home is always exhilarating, and the chastised returnees participated in the realization of Jeremiah's prophecy.

Seventy years had been a long time to wait. Why so long? Could not the Lord have accomplished His purpose in less time? And why do all of us have to endure the long vigils before some unsatisfactory things are solved—or perhaps not even corrected at all in this life?

Waiting, trusting, believing, patiently enduring, is the only formula that refines difficult human nature. I often watched the washermen of India pounding clothes on rocks beside a stream of water. Then they pounded with a paddle—anything to agitate and loosen the dirt and stain. A washing machine employs the same principle.

The slow process of growth and accomplishment extends the refining method of test and trial. Robert Collyer commented, "The days which Job wrestled with his dark maladies are the only days that make him worth remembrance." Jesus said, "But he that shall endure unto the end, the same shall be saved" (Matthew 24:13, KJV).

After God told Abraham he would have an heir, more than twenty-five years passed before the joyful cry of the promised child gladdened the camp. When old age made the promise physically impossible, the patriarch still had to wait patiently and believe God. Why? Well, that was part of the necessary schooling Abraham needed. Only God knew why; but a good reason, which impatient men fail to comprehend, lay behind the long wait. Let the Pilot bring the ship in; it is not for the passengers to question the compass and chart.

Without the seventy years in captivity there would not have been the glory of some great Bible epics. Daniel, Esther, Mordecai, would not have come out of the ease and comfort of Palestine. Why seventy years were required to accomplish God's purpose instead of a lesser period is something only He knows. But He still took care of His children during the bitter years of captivity—that is all we need to know.

Patient waiting tries the soul but sharpens the spirit. Nothing in nature comes by sudden jerks or instant bounds. Listen to the message of the earth. The little seed slowly upheaves its way until the ground parts, and the blade stands up to greet the sun. The germs of valor and faith must also have their silent undergrowth. But as sure as there's a providence which makes the flowers appear, there will be the blossoms of the soul.

Be patient, as were the exiles in Babylon who turned to God in their distress. Be patient like the grain of wheat. Day after day it slowly grows until the head is full. Everything—whether man, beast, or plant—must silently and patiently mature.

Patient endurance amid suffering, correction for our follies and pride, only prepare us for the day of going home. Says the new Jeremiah after pronouncing the judgments of the divine:

"It is good to wait in patience and sigh

for deliverance by the Lord" (Lamentations 3:26, NEB).

Unlike Jeremiah, we give up too soon. Deliverance is delayed for a good reason, but impatience mars our response. Many great accomplishments have been won by just persevering when it seemed logical to quit. "Where there is an open mind, there will always be a frontier," said Charles F. Kettering.

A glowing oil bonanza lies on America's energy frontier along the North Slope of Alaska. Search for oil began at Prudhoe Bay in 1963 when British Petroleum and Atlantic Richfield started drilling. By 1968 British Petroleum had spent $30 million on dry holes and decided to stop searching. Atlantic Richfield had spent $125 million without a single producer.

"Quit" seemed to be the opinion of the directors. But some persistent people within the company held out for just one more try. They prevailed. That well was the big strike, and the great rush began.

Some people, after a few attempts to gain eternal life, get as close to the great prize as the Prudhoe Bay oil episode, then are tempted to give up, but they make a final effort which spells success. They can be certain of one never-failing fact: Christ will always hold the rope that keeps them from falling into oblivion.

English botanists, searching for rare flowers in Switzerland, saw some beautiful specimens down on the side of a precipice. They asked a boy to go down with a rope, which they would hold, tied around him. The boy told them to wait a few minutes and went away. In a short time he returned with his father. "If my father holds the rope," he said, "I will go down."

We can safely go anywhere or wait patiently when the big steady hands of God hold the rope. He has never failed anyone, and He certainly does not intend to break His record with you or me.

Jeremiah held on when it was incredibly hard to hold on. Battered and bruised, lacerated and maligned, he refused to give up when logic indicated otherwise. He thereby gained the favor of heaven and an indescribably wonderful eternity. What were a few years of test and trial beside the endless billions packed with everlasting joys and thrilling excitement in Paradise?

So we gather the equipment that trials patiently endured provide, and the final call to go home finds us ready.

"Let him turn his cheek to the smiter
    and endure full measure of abuse;
  for the Lord will not cast off
    his servants for ever.
  He may punish cruelly, yet he will have compassion
    in the fullness of his love;

he does not willingly afflict
>   or punish any mortal man" (verses 30-33, NEB).

Jeremiah speaks to the children of God today from the fire and tribulation of his time, and the word shines upon them with the inner peace of the born again. They have an incontestable legitimacy to the homeland, transcending every earthly allurement. Rejecting the backsliding, compromising, pleasure-seeking ways of the old Judeans, these New Jerusalem homesteaders can say, "I've tried this sin-riddled way, and I like the other much better."

Instead of a perpetual motion in futility, with no rhyme or reason for the troubles of life, Jeremiah, viewed in new perspective, is an explanation of why things happen. Evil gets us into trouble. For the pure in heart God uses the mystifying struggles to regenerate and cleanse. Then comes the Restoration, an earthly confirmation such as Israel's return to the homeland at the end of the seventy years. To the Christian believer it is restoration, here and now, by the redemption of Christ. Finally we share the grand jubilee: the complete, ultimate restoration at the second coming of Christ! Then the spiritual Israelites—the redeemed of all time—go home to the paradise of the New Jerusalem. This is the song of the new Jeremiah.

>   "They shall come with shouts of joy to Zion's height,
>   shining with happiness at the bounty of the Lord. . . .
>   They shall become like a watered garden
>   and they shall never want again. . . .
>   I will turn their mourning into gladness. . . .
>   This is the very word of the Lord" (31:12-14, NEB).

The plan and purpose of God will then be complete. Jeremiah, the bold and fearless, the incorruptible, guides us to the immaculate homeland. We're going home, going to the untarnished house of joy.